OCR Computing for AS Level
F452 - Programming Techniques and Logical Methods
A Revision Guide

Alan Milosevic, Dorothy Williams

Published by Bagatelle Publications Ltd 2012

Published by Bagatelle Publications Ltd

http://www.bagatelle.com/

First published 2012

Printed in the United Kingdom

Set using LaTeX. Font 9pt Minion Pro.

Contents

Introduction

This revision guide has been written specifically to support work done throughout the year in F452 - Programming Techniques and Logical Methods. It is not intended to replace a good text book but when used properly will provide an excellent supplement. The revision guide is divided into chapters and sections. Each chapter and section reflect divisions in the original OCR specification for F452. Notes are distributed throughout the guide usually immediately after each section heading. These notes are then followed by a range of questions taken directly from OCR past papers, together with the examiner's mark scheme solutions. In many cases the notes are minimal since the examiner's solutions provide excellent notes.

All of the questions are taken from OCR past papers. In each instance the question number and paper are displayed together with the number of marks awarded for a fully correct answer. The answers are provided by the OCR mark scheme for the particular paper. Many of these answers are given in bullet point form. You should assume that each bullet point is worth one mark, with the proviso that if the bullet point contains an ellipsis (...), the text following the ellipsis expanding upon or providing an explanation for the first part of the text is also worth one mark.

The student who works his or her way through this book carefully reading the notes and the past paper questions and answers will give themselves an excellent opportunity to consolidate and review the material learned during the course.

Designing solutions to problems

1.1 DISCUSS THE IMPORTANCE OF GOOD INTERFACE DESIGN

Good interface design is essential if users are to make best use of a given piece of software. Modern smartphones exemplify good interface design. In the main the software applications are intuitive, easy to learn, and display information in a simple, consistent fashion. Well designed interfaces are informative, efficient, clear and depending on interface type, use sensible interface elements such as drop down menus, labels, text boxes, radio buttons and check boxes. Badly designed interfaces are typically non-intuitive, inconsistent and difficult to use.

For high marks on these types of questions, answers need to be concise, accurate and use technical terms correctly.

Sanchez is a student doing his A-Level Computing project. He is working with a recruiting agency which specialises in local part-time jobs for students. The agency wants a program which will allow the user to add details of a student to a file, add details of a job to another file and match students with jobs.

When a student registers with the agency for part-time work, they must fill in a form giving the following information: name, date of birth, mobile telephone number and whether they have a full driving licence. Using this as well as other examples, discuss the importance of a good design of the interface used to input data into a computer program. [F452 Q2 Jan 2011 (8)]

Points to be made may include:

- The UI should be effective i.e. all the data required can be input accurately
- The data capture form can help by ensuring data is already in format to be input
- ...e.g. boxes can be supplied for individual characters/format of date of birth/telephone numbers
- ...and clear instructions to users
- As a result, the agency will not lose contacts of students resulting in potential loss of business
- The UI should be efficient i.e. make best use of available resources
- ...the input screen should be in the same order as the data capture form
- ...as this does not waste staff time finding the data on the form
- Use of user interface tools like drop downs and check boxes (e.g. for driving license)

- This maximises throughput of data entry ultimately saving money for the agency

A computing student has written a program which stores and prints recipes. The program has a graphical user interface (GUI). Describe how a good design of the GUI can make the program easier to use. [F452 Q1 Jan 2009 (4)]

- Easier to learn … due to familiar layout … and good use of online help
- Will be intuitive
- Fewer mistakes will be made when using the program
- Input will be faster
- Use of GUI objects such as drop downs/option buttons
- Dialogue boxes to alert on validation errors
- No information overload / sensitive to the needs of the user

1.2   DESIGN AND DOCUMENT DATA CAPTURE FORMS, SCREEN AND REPORT LAYOUTS

The recipe data entry screen allows the user to enter the following data about each recipe.
  - **The name of the recipe (e.g. Sponge Cake)**
  - **The number of people the recipe caters for (e.g. 6)**
  - **A table of the ingredients of the recipe with 3 columns**
    - **the name of the ingredient (e.g. flour)**
    - **the quantity required (e.g. 300)**
    - **the units in which the quantity required is measured (e.g. grams).**
On the blank screen below, show a suitable layout for the data entry screen. (8)

In this question, the examiners gave marks for the following …

- There is a title
- The end user can enter the name of recipe
- The end user can enter the Number catered for

- For each ingredient:
    - The end user can enter the Name of ingredient
    - The end user can enter the Quantity of ingredient
    - The end user can enter the Unit of ingredient
- Unit can be entered by a dropdown list … which has been populated with some common values

- There is a facility for scrolling for more ingredients than the screen can fit

- There is a button to start over/clear data
- There is a button to save ingredient data/add a line of ingredients
- There is a button to close the program

- Optimal use of screen
- Space for ingredient and recipe name long enough (at least 10 characters)

In questions of this nature, make sure that you use the whole screen and very importantly, that you have appropriate interface elements for all of the data needed. Space your elements out sensibly. If the interface requires the user to enter data make sure that you have allocated sufficient space for the data. For example, if the form requires the user to enter his or her name, make it clear to the examiner that you are allocating sufficient space for a user's name with perhaps 15 characters. As in the previous example it would make sense to include buttons to reset data entry, to close the program and to save the recipe. Try to imagine that you are using such a program. What would you see on screen? Draw what you would see. Visualise!

Here is another example.

Wayne is writing an application for a touch screen mobile phone to identify types of ladybird.

The application will have a single interface which has a facility to input the size of the ladybird in mm a facility to input the number of spots (1-30) a facility to input the colour of the spots (BLACK, WHITE, RED or OTHER) an output to short short descriptions of the types of ladybird fitting the criteria which have been input.

In the outline below draw a design for the interface of this application. You may annotate your design to explain how it works. [F452 Q1 Jun 2011 (8)]

The examiners will expect the design to include :

- Suitable title AND generally good use of space
- A method for entering the size, number and colour of spots
- A method for entering either numeric value (size or number of spots) is suitable for touch screen interface (e.g. drop-down, spinner, numeric software keyboard)
- A method for entering colour of spots is suitable for touch screen interface (e.g. drop down, menu, radio buttons, tickboxes)
- Command button (or similar) to initiate search
- Clear/reset/close button
- Area for output of picture of ladybird
- Area for outputting the name of the ladybird
- Area for output of textual description
- Facility to deal with more than 1 match

You may be given a diagram of a simple interface and asked to justify why one particular interface element is being used as in the following question.

A computer program is designed to store the results of matches in a football competition and calculate the rankings of the teams.

To enter the results of each match, an interface will allow the user to select the name of two teams from drop down lists, and enter the number of goals scored in corresponding text boxes.

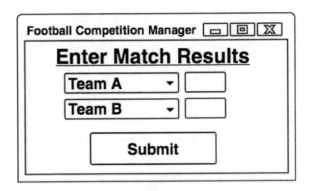

Explain the advantages of using a drop down list to enter the name of a team. [F452 Q1 Jun 2010 (4)]

In this question, the examiner is looking for insight into how use of interface elements might help with validation and also avoid errors. The examiners were expecting answers along the following lines.

Any 4 of :

- Used for validation
- …as it provides an existence check/ to ensure that only teams in the competition can be entered
- Prevents typing errors
- …such as being entered as a different team
- Allows faster input
- …as the operator does not need to type in the name of the team

When a student registers with an agency for part-time work, they must fill in a form giving the following information.

- **Name**
- **Date of birth**
- **Mobile telephone number**
- **Whether they have a full driving licence**

In the space below, design the layout of a data capture form the student would complete. [F452 Q2 Jan 2011 (8)]

The examiners were quite specific in their requirements for this question. You would get marks for the following.

- Title
- Appropriate instructions (e.g. Use block capitals)
- Name can be entered …as separate Surname & Other names
- Date of birth can be entered …in a specified format
- Mobile phone number can be entered …in a specified format
- Driving Licence can be entered …as a tick-box, YES/NO etc …

As a final example of this type of question, in the specimen paper the examiners posed the following question.

An electronic general knowledge game displays, on the screen, the following:

- **a question**
- **four possible answers**
- **a clock to allow a set amount of time to answer the question**
- **a score (which is added to if the question is answered correctly)**
- **the score required in order to win the game**

The player touches the answer that they want to input as their choice. On the blank screen below, show a suitable layout to present the five areas. [F452 Q1 Specimen Questions (7)]

In the mark scheme answer to this question, the examiners provided a simple diagram of how they felt a student might have placed all the necessary components, together with suggestions for how the marks should be awarded. Firstly, how the marks should be awarded.

- Area shown for question
- areas shown for all 4 answers
- area for clock/timer
- area for current score
- area for target score
- each answer area is big enough to accommodate touch
- no unreasonable blank areas

Now the diagram.

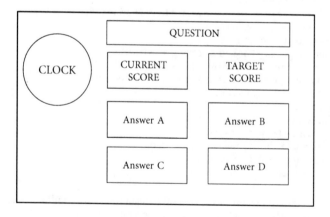

1.3   DETERMINE THE DATA REQUIREMENTS OF A PROGRAM

See section 3.8 on page 53.

1.4   EXPLAIN THE ADVANTAGES OF TOP-DOWN/MODULAR DESIGN

For reasons of efficiency and of simply being able to get a clear understanding of a complex problem, it is invariably necessary to split it up into smaller modules. These modules can be split again and again until you end up with modules that can be coded quickly and straightforwardly as functions in your programming language of choice. As the questions and answers below explain, the advantages are pretty clear.

However, there are some consequences of this approach that will need to be borne in mind by the designers. Separate modules will have to be joined (the technical term is *linked*) together to make the final program. It is possible that if the modules have not been properly designed and implemented, one or modules might have variable names that will clash with each other. Additionally it's often the case that functions written in one module will make use of functions in other modules, usually by passing and receiving parameters. Clearly if the modules are to work correctly the documentation describing these functions must be written and adhered to. We call this the *interface* between the modules. Finally, once all of the modules have been linked, system wide testing will need to be carried out to check that everything works as intended.

Describe TWO advantages of using a modular design to produce software. [F452 Q2 Jun 2010 (4)]

- Each module is a small part of the problem/focuses on a small sub-task
- ...and so easy to solve
- ...and test/debug
- ...easy to maintain/update a part of the system
- ...as the program will be well structured
- ...with clearly defined interfaces
- ...without affecting the rest
- Development can be shared between a team of programmers
- ...so program developed faster
- ...easier to monitor progress
- ...modules can be allocated according to expertise
- ...improving the quality of the final product
- Different modules can be programmed in different languages
- ...suitable for the application
- ...good example
- Reduces the amount of code that needs to be produced
- ...because code can be reused
- ...or standard library modules can be used
- ...reducing time of development
- ...good example

A company decides to produce the program using a top-down modular design. Explain what is meant by a top-down design. [F452 Q4 Specimen Question Paper (2)]

- Problem is split into smaller sub-problems
- ...which, in turn, are split into smaller sub-problems
- ...until each is one element of the algorithm

State three advantages and one disadvantage of dividing a problem into modules for coding. (4)

Advantages

- Smaller problems are easier to solve/understand
- ...and easier to test
- ...and easier to debug
- Development can be shared between a team of programmers
- ...according to individual strengths
- use of library modules
- code can be reused

Disadvantages

- Modules must be linked
- Programmers must ensure that cross-referencing is done
- Interfaces between modules must be planned
- Testing of links must be carried out

1.5 MODULAR DESIGN USING STRUCTURE DIAGRAMS AND STEPWISE REFINEMENT

Good programmers make use of a variety of techniques to design solutions to complex tasks. One such is stepwise-refinement, which is as discussed earlier, the splitting of complex tasks into simpler and smaller units until each is simple and small enough to be coded with relatively little difficulty. Another common technique is the use of structure diagrams which provide a simple visual description of the decomposition of more complex tasks. The following questions illustrate the type of questions you might expect.

Explain what is meant by stepwise refinement. [F452 Q2 Jun 2010 (3)]

- Each module/task is defined in simple terms
- ...and then split into a number of smaller sub-modules/sub-tasks
- ...which are successively split
- ...until each is small enough to be programmed

Sanchez is a student doing his A-Level Computing project. He is working with a recruiting agency which specialises in local part-time jobs for students.

The agency wants a program which will allow the user to

- **add details of a student to a file**
- **add details of a job to another file**
- **match students with jobs**

Sanchez decides to produce a top-down design for the program. Part of this design is shown in the structure diagram below.

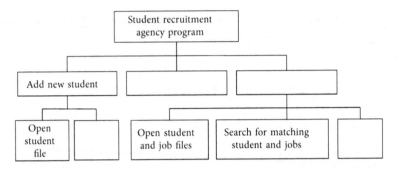

Write the letters A, B, C and D in the blank boxes to show the most appropriate location for the following modules.

- **A = Add new job**
- **B = Append student record**
- **C = Match students to jobs**
- **D = Print report of matches**

[F452 Q2 Jan 2011 (4)]

Answer :

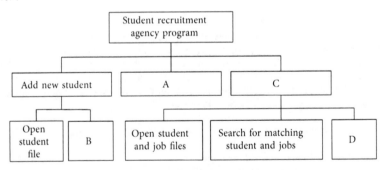

A telephone company is producing software to calculate the bills for its customers. A text file which contains a list of the calls for the customer is used. An extract of this file is given below.

Date	Time	Number	Duration
01/01/2007	00:01	0202332981	1:04
01/01/2007	00:23	0121928192	29:52
02/01/2007	07:45	0870736728	112:19

The company operates a flat rate so that the cost of calls depends only on the duration, and not on the destination number or the time of day. The company decides to produce the program using a top-down modular design. The development team decides to divide the problem into four modules as shown in the diagram below. Extend the diagram by dividing the module Get Total Duration into further sub-modules. Do not attempt to divide any of the other modules further. [F452 Q4 Specimen Question Paper (4)]

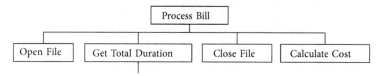

To get the total duration you're going to have to declare and initialise a variable to hold the total duration (totalDuration might be a good candidate) and then read the file line by line, extracting the duration each time and adding it to totalDuration. The examiner wanted something along the following lines.

- Initialise total
- Read a line of data
- Extract duration
- Add duration to total
- Attempt at a further layer
- Candidates attempt shows horizontal order

Visually, they expected something like.

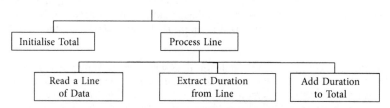

A section of the software allows the user to search for songs from a database and produce a list of selected songs. This section contains the following modules.

- **A module to enter search criteria**
- **A module to search the database**
  - **by artist**

    ◦ **by title**
    ◦ **by type**

A module to display the results of the search A module to add a song from the search results to the list of songs to be included on the CD Part of the top-down design for this section is shown below. Complete this top-down design to show the modules listed above. [F452 Q2 Jun 2010 (7)]

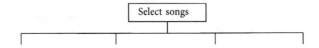

Answer :

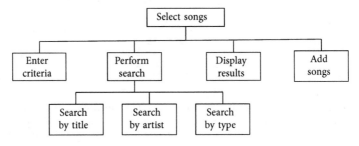

Marks are awarded :

- For each box under Select Song
- For the boxes under select song being in the right order
- For the three boxes under search the database
- For no incorrect lines

1.6 PRODUCE ALGORITHMS TO SOLVE PROBLEMS

We now come to the whole raison d'être of Computer Science, i.e. the creation of algorithms to solve problems. Unsurprisingly, the examiners want to make sure that you, the student is familiar with working with algorithms. This means reading, correcting, enhancing and creating them.

The specification requires you to be familiar with using *flow charts* and *pseudo code* to express an algorithm. It also needs you to be able to *evaluate them by commenting on their efficiency, correctness and appropriateness for the problem to be solved.* The examples from past papers together with the notes that follow, should give you a clear idea of what is required.

The first example is a case of modifying a simple algorithm.

A computer program is designed to store the results of matches in a football competition and calculate the ranking of the teams. When the results are entered, the number of points of each team are updated as follows.

- If both teams have the same number of goals (draw) then each team gets 1 point.
- If one team has more goals than the other (i.e. there is a winner) then the winning team gets 3 points, and the losing team gets 0 points.

The algorithm for updating points in the case of a draw is given below.

```
IF   goals_of_first_team = goals_of_second_team THEN
   points_of(first_team) = points_of(first_team) + 1
  points_of(second_team) = points_of(second_team) + 1
END IF
```

Using the same format, write the algorithm for updating the points if there is a winner.
[F452 Q1 Jun 2010 (4)]

Answer

```
IF goals_of_first_team > goals_of_second_team THEN
 points_of(first_team) = points_of(first_team) + 3
ELSEIF goals_of_second_team > goals_of_first_team THEN
     points_of(second_team) = points_of(second_team) + 3
END IF
```

This example simply needs you to use the > sign appropriately to increment the winning team's points score by 3.

A more complex question, similar examples of which are usually worth 8 marks is shown below.

A theatre has 10 rows, labelled A to J from front to back, and 15 seats in each row, numbered 1 to 15 from left to right.

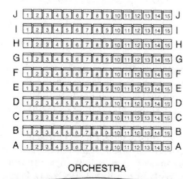

ORCHESTRA

STAGE

The program uses the following rules to choose the best seats.

Rule 1: All seats in one booking must be in the same row, next to each other.
Rule 2: The seats must be as close to the front as possible.

Write an algorithm which takes the number of tickets wanted as an input, and outputs the best seats available. [F452 Q4 Jun 09 (8)]

As a first step you are going to have to find out how many tickets you are going to need (which presumably should be at least 1 and less than 15). Once you have that information you should check whether there are a sufficient number of seats together in the first row. If so, problem solved, else you're going to have to check the second row and so on until either you have found a contiguous set of seats or there simply aren't any in which case you should tell the user. To check that the seats are together you should first find an empty seat and then check that the next n-1 seats in the row are also empty.

The examiners expected you to provide a solution written in either pseudo code or as a flowchart that included the following points.

- Input NumberOfTickets, n
- If $n < 0$ or $n > 15$ produce an error message
- And stop
- (Else)
- Loop through the rows from Row A
- Until seats are found
- ...or you reach row J
- (provided this is within a loop)
- Test that there are n seats available in row (together)
- ...E.g. by finding first empty seat
- ...and checking $n - 1$ seats after it.
- If seats found then output the seat numbers

1.7   DESCRIBE THE STEPS OF AN ALGORITHM USING A PROGRAM FLOWCHART

Questions regarding flowcharts either require you to create your own or alternatively, to read one given to you and to make some judgment as to what goes in any missing spots. If you are asked to create your own, ideally you'd have an ellipse at the start saying "Start" and another at the end saying "Stop". In between you should use parallelograms to indicate input and output, rectangles for steps in the program and diamonds to indicate choices between yes and no (or true or false). Some examples of questions using or requiring flow charts are shown below.

A company organises a mobile phone quiz. Players are sent a multiple-choice question by text message. If they answer correctly the next question is sent. If the answer is wrong, they are eliminated. Players who answer 20 questions correctly win a prize. When a player receives a question, they must reply by sending A, B, C or D. Part of the process for checking the answer is described below.

- **The computer checks whether the answer matches the correct answer**
- **If the answer is correct it checks whether the player has answered 20 questions**
- **If the player has answered 20 questions it replies with the message"You have won a prize"**
- **If the answer was correct but the player has not answered 20 questions then it replies with the next question**

- If the answer does not match the correct answer it records that the player is eliminated in the player file and replies with the message "Wrong answer. You are Eliminated"

Complete the flow chart below to show this part of the process. [F452 Q3 Jun 2011 (5)]

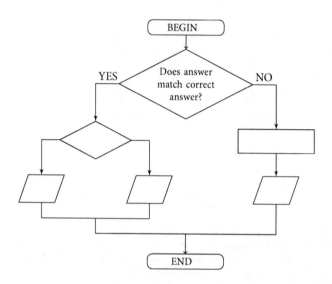

In this question, if the player has answered correctly the algorithm needs to check whether they have completed 20 questions so the empty diamond must check that this is the case. If they have, a message to the effect "You've won a prize" can be displayed. If not, the player should be asked the next question. If however the player had not entered the correct answer the player should be eliminated from the file and a message to that effect sent back to the player.

With these points in mind, the completed flowchart will look like the following.

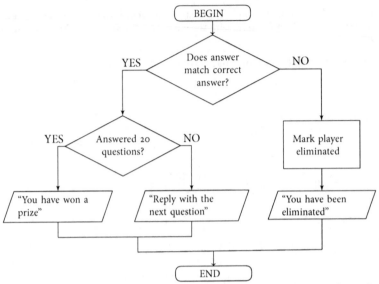

The next question asks the student to read an algorithm expressed in the form of a flow chart and for two sets of input to work out what the result will be.

A 10-pin bowling club uses a computer program to rank its members according to their bowling average. The computer places the members into three different categories, Beginner, Improver and Pro according to the data in their record. The method used to decide which category a member belongs to is given in the flowchart below.

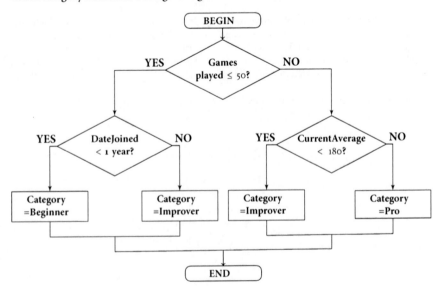

The records of two members on 1 January 2010 are shown below. For each member, state in which category they will be placed, explaining how you obtain your answer from the flowchart. [F452 Q1 Jan 2010 (3,3)]

> **MemberID:** A6718
> **Name:** Bashir Ali
> **DateJoined:** 03/042/2008
> **CurrentAverage:** 200
> **GamesPlayed** = 40

- "GamesPlayed ≤ 50" is TRUE (so take left branch)
- "DateJoined < 1 year ago" is FALSE (so take right branch)
- Consequently, Category = Improver

> **MemberID:** S9140
> **Name:** Susan Striker
> **DateJoined:** 01/03/2000
> **CurrentAverage:** 180
> **GamesPlayed** = 320

- "GamesPlayed ≤ 50" is FALSE (so take right branch)
- "CurrentAverage < 180" is FALSE (so take right branch)
- Consequently, Category = Pro

The club changes the rules. **Complete the flowchart at the arrow marked * to show: If the CurrentAverage ≥ 200 then the category should be Pro, otherwise the category should be Improver. (6)**

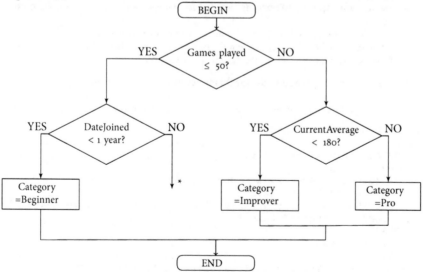

- CurrentAverage ≥ 200 (or equivalent) at * ... in a rhombus

- YES and NO labels are present
- Category = Pro for correct branch/if CurrentAverage ≥ 200
- Category = Improver for correct branch/if CurrentAverage < 200
- Flowchart reconnected correctly
- Include diagram

The appropriate addition to the flowchart should therefore be.

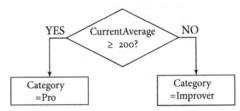

1.8   DESCRIBE THE STEPS OF AN ALGORITHM USING PSEUDO-CODE

The examiners often do ask you to use pseudo-code rather than real code when writing algorithms. This gives you plenty of flexibility and you don't need to produce the exact syntax of any particular programming language. However, you do need to be rigorous in your thinking. The example below is typical of the type of question you might get.

A program handling a cash point machine (ATM) contains the function GetAmountWanted. A description of this function is given below.

- **It prompts the user to input the amount to withdraw**
- **The amount input by the user is checked to make sure that it can be dispensed in £10 notes**
- **If this is possible, the function returns the amount input by the user**
- **If it is not possible, the user is given the option to input a different amount or cancel**
- **If the user chooses to cancel, the function returns the number -1**

Write an algorithm, in pseudo-code, for this function. [F452 Q2 Jun 2011 (8)]

Appropriate pseudo-code supplied by the examiners is shown below.

```
FUNCTION GetAmountWanted()
  REPEAT
    OUTPUT 'Please enter amount'
    INPUT Amount
    IF Amount <= 0 OR Amount MOD 10 <> 0
      AmountIsValid = FALSE
      OUTPUT 'That amount is invalid. Would you like to cancel?'
      INPUT UserWantsToCancel
    ELSE
      AmountIsValid = TRUE
    END IF
  UNTIL AmountIsValid = TRUE OR UserWantsToCancel = TRUE
  IF AmountIsValid = TRUE THEN
    RETURN Amount
```

```
    ELSE
        RETURN -1
    END IF
END FUNCTION
```

The examiners are looking for your pseudo-code to cover the following points.

- Loops until amount is valid or user chooses to cancel

Within the loop

- Output request for amount to withdraw
- Input amount
- If amount is divisible by 10
- Return amount (this could be after the loop)
- Else output question to restart or cancel ... and input users response
- if user cancelled return -1 (this could be after the loop)

The gears of a bicycle contain up to 8 rings with decreasing numbers of teeth. A computer program in a bicycle repair shop allows the user to input the number of teeth on each ring into an array called Ring using the method described below.

- **The user inputs the number of rings between 1 and 8.**
- **The user then inputs the number of teeth on each ring, starting with the largest.**
- **The program checks that each number of teeth input is smaller than the previous number.**
- **The program stores the number of teeth on the first ring into the array Ring as Ring(1), the number of teeth on the second ring as Ring(2) and so on.**
- **If there are fewer than 8 rings, any unused elements of the array Ring are set to 0.**

Write an algorithm for the routine to input the number of teeth on each ring as described above. [F452 Q4 Jan 2011 (8)]

The examiners expected the following algorithm to include the following.

- Input number of rings
- The number input must be between 1 and 8
- ...give an appropriate error message if it isn't
- Uses a loop set from 1 (or from 2 if 1 dealt with separately)
- ...to the number of rings
- (Within the loop)
- ...Input number of teeth
- ...Check that the number of teeth < number of teeth for previous ring
- ...but does not check this for the first

An algorithm that would get you full marks might read something like this. We start by initialising all elements of the Ring array to zero. This saves us having to set any unused elements to zero later (although this isn't mentioned in the mark scheme).

```
FOR (i = 1 to 8)
    Ring(i) = 0
INPUT noRings
WHILE ((noRings<1) or (noRings>8))
    PRINT 'Error - number of rings must be between 1 and 8'
```

```
READ the first ring size into Ring(1)
ringIndex = 2
REPEAT
  READ nextRing
  Ring(ringIndex) = nextRing
  WHILE (Ring(ringIndex) >= Ring(ringIndex-1))
    PRINT 'Please enter a ring size smaller than the previous size'
    READ nextRing
    Ring(ringIndex) = nextRing
  END WHILE
  ringIndex = ringIndex + 1
UNTIL all ring sizes have been input
```

A printing company uses a computer program to randomly generate and print bingo tickets. Each bingo ticket has a grid with three rows and nine columns. Each row contains 5 numbers and 4 blank spaces. The computer program stores the numbers in a 2-dimensional array called Ticket. In the array Ticket, the first index represents the row and the second represents the column. e.g. Ticket(1,4) = 32 means the number on row 1, column 4 is 32.

To generate the tickets, the computer program first fills in the columns with random integers. After filling the array, the computer program ensures that no numbers have been repeated, and replaces four positions on each row with the number 0.

A bingo ticket is printed using the following method.

- For every row in the array
- For every column in that row

    - If the value is 0 then output a space
    - otherwise output the value

Write an algorithm in pseudo-code to print the numbers in the array onto a ticket. You should indent your pseudo-code correctly to make it easier to understand. [F452 Q3 Jun 2010 (8)]

Pseudo-code supplied by the examiners is shown below.

```
FOR Row = 1 TO 3
  FOR Column = 1 TO 9
    IF Ticket(Row, Column) = 0 THEN
      PRINT ' '
    ELSE
      PRINT Ticket(Row, Column)
    END IF
  NEXT Column
  Go to new line
NEXT ROW
```

The examiners are looking for code that meets the following bullet points.

- Correct row loop
- Correct column loop
- Correctly nested/considers every element of the array Ticket
- Checks if the value is zero and

- ...prints a space if it is zero
- ...prints the value if it is not zero
- There is a new line at the end of each row
- Correct indentation has been used

A mail order company charges for delivery depending on the volume and the weight of the items purchased. A computer program processes orders and calculates the cost of delivery. The cost of delivery is calculated as follows.

- There is a basic delivery charge of £5 for all orders
- If the total weight of an order is more than 1kg, there is an additional charge of £0.50 for every extra 0.1kg.
- If the total volume of an order is more than 1000cm³, there is an additional charge of £0.50 for every extra 200cm³.

Write an algorithm for a function which makes use of the global variables TotalWeight and TotalVolume and returns the cost of delivery. [F452 Q4 Jan 2010 (7)]

Example (supplied by the examiners)

```
FUNCTION CostOfDelivery()
   IF TotalWeight > 1 THEN
       ExtraWeight = TotalWeight-1
       ExtraWeightUnits = ExtraWeight DIV 0.1
       ExtraWeightCost = ExtraWeightUnits * 0.5
   ELSE
       ExtraWeightCost = 0
   END IF

   IF TotalVolume > 1000 THEN
       ExtraVolume = TotalVolume-1000
       ExtraVolumeUnits = ExtraVolume DIV 200
       ExtraVolumeCost = ExtraVolumeUnits * 0.5
   ELSE
       ExtraVolumeCost = 0
END IF
   CostOfDelivery = 5 + ExtraVolumeCost + ExtraWeightCost
END FUNCTION
```

Clearly your algorithm may be different so the examiners were looking for the following points which any correct algorithm would be expected to incorporate.

- An algorithm for a function which returns the cost of delivery (incorrect calculations can be accepted, provided the function returns the result of the calculations)
- The variables TotalWeight and TotalVolume are used in the calculations (as global variables or as parameters of the function)
- Determines amount of excess weight if any
- Determines cost of excess weight
- Determines amount of excess volume if any
- Determines cost of excess volume
- Correctly calculates cost of delivery

The only way to become truly effective and efficient at writing algorithms is to simply to write lots of them. During the AS year you will have been taught how to write software in some appropriate high level language. You will have been asked to use the language to solve problems. These problems are invariably best expressed first in a combination of flow charts and pseudo-code. Only when the problem is clearly understood and a possible solution sketched out as a flow chart or in pseudo-code should you start trying to code the solution. You might think that this is long winded and it would be quicker to simply sit down at the computer and start coding. Except with the most trivial problems you would be wrong. Taking time to understand the problem fully by expressing it as a flow chart or in pseudo-code invariably leads to solutions that are implemented quicker and are more robust when first tested.

1.9   Understand, implement and evaluate algorithms

Questions on this section of the syllabus usually check that you can read an algorithm properly and can spot errors in the logic, for example when FOR and WHILE loops are incorrectly nested as in the artificial example below.

```
FOR i = 1 to 20
  WHILE x < 10
    P = Q
    Q = Q + 1
NEXT i
  ENDWHILE
```

Often you are given an algorithm and are required to evaluate it for a number of different possible inputs. These are usually not terribly difficult but the examiner will expect to see exactly how you worked through the algorithm as in the following example.

A television talent contest allows the audience to vote for one of three contestants, A, B or C, using a voting pad. The following algorithm is written to determine which of A, B and C gets the highest vote.

```
01 IF VOTES(1) > VOTES(2) THEN
02    IF VOTES(1) > VOTES(3) THEN
03       OUTPUT 'A'
04    ELSE
05       OUTPUT 'C'
06    ENDIF
07 ELSE
08    IF VOTES(2) > VOTES(3) THEN
09       OUTPUT 'B'
10    ELSE
11       OUTPUT 'C'
12    ENDIF
13 ENDIF
```

Some people do not vote and the result of a particular vote is that all of A, B and C receive equal votes. State the line numbers that will be executed by the algorithm and which of A, B or C will be output. [F452 Q3 Specimen Questions (4)]

- 1,7
- 8,10
- 11,12,13

- C

Explain how the algorithm would need to be altered to deal with two or three of the options receiving equal votes. Do not produce the algorithm. (4)

- Check if all 3 equal
- ...output suitable response/output All equal scores
- ...check if two are equal
- ...three times to cover the three possible pairs
- ...IF the third vote is smaller

Although you are not required to produce the algorithm, it is a useful revision exercise to do so. The following code snippet will test whether all three are equal and if so, will produce an appropriate message. If all three are not the same, it checks whether any of the three possible pairs are the same, outputting an appropriate message if they are. Finally if none of the previous conditions were met a message indicating that all received different numbers of votes is output.

```
01 IF VOTES(1) = VOTES(2) THEN
02    IF VOTES(1) = VOTES(3) THEN
03       OUTPUT 'All three votes are equal'
04    ELSE
05       OUTPUT 'Votes for A and B are equal'
06    ENDIF
07 ELSE
08    IF VOTES(1) = VOTES(3) THEN
09       OUTPUT 'Votes for A and C are equal'
10    ELSE
11       IF VOTES(2) = VOTES(3) THEN
12          OUTPUT 'Votes for B and C are equal'
13       ELSE
14          OUTPUT 'Votes are all different'
15       ENDIF
16    ENDIF
17 ENDIF
```

Note that in lines 01, 02, 08 and 11 the code used the equals (=) sign to test whether two values are the same. As mentioned elsewhere in this revision guide many languages distinguish between between assignment and comparison. In this example we are comparing. Languages such as C, C++ and Java use a double equal sign for comparisons (==) and a single equals sign for assignment. Pascal uses := for assignment and a single equals sign for comparison. Care should always be taken and many a novice (and some not such novices) have tripped themselves up over this distinction.

1.10   DESCRIBE THE USE OF RAPID APPLICATION DEVELOPMENT

Rapid Application Development (RAD) is a software design strategy which includes prototyping and iterative development. It has a number of significant advantages over the traditional waterfall and spiral models. In traditional models the user is rarely consulted beyond the early analysis stage and since traditional models often take a long time to produce an end result, user needs and specifications can change so much that the project fails to produce a final solution. In contrast, the RAD approach involves the user throughout the project. Prototypes of a solution are developed very early in the development cycle. These prototypes are discussed with the user and any modifications or enhancements can be added as the solution develops. More sophisticated prototypes are developed, more discussions ensue and the process continues until both user and developer are happy with the resulting solution. There are clear advantages to involving the user throughout the process. The user sees the development proceeding, they can introduce modifications to the specification without excessive increases both to cost and development time and project milestones can be set by which the developer can be paid and the user's confidence maintained.

The only significant disadvantage to having a user involved throughout the development process is that it can lead to unrealistic expectations on the part of the user. Seeing working prototypes early on can lead to a false sense of how long the project is likely to take and additionally it can lead to users changing specifications almost on a whim.

A company uses Rapid Application Development (RAD) to develop software. Describe RAD and state one advantage of using it. [F452 Q2 Jan 2009 (3)]

- RAD is a method for designing software
- Where a Prototype design
- ...with reduced functionality is produced
- Then tested and evaluated
- ...to refine the design of the next prototype
- This is repeated (with a more refined prototype each time)
- ...until Prototype is accepted
- ...until final product is produced

Advantages

- Something can be seen working early in the project
- End user more involved / can change the requirements as product becomes clearer
- Overall development time is quicker (than alternative methods)

Rapid Application Development (RAD) is to be used in the development of some software. Explain how the use of RAD can speed up the development process. F452 Q3 Specimen Questions (2)]

- Prototypes of the software are produced
- ...which have reduced functionality
- ...and can be produced quickly

Explain how the end user is involved during the testing and refining of the software. (2)

- Prototypes are tested/evaluated with the end user
- Outcome is used to inform the next prototype
- Process is repeated/iterative development
- ...until a final product is produced

Describe two advantages, for the user, of using a RAD approach (4)

- End user can see a working prototype sooner/can see something happening
- End user is involved in the design/can influence the direction the program is taking
- Overall development time is shorter/reducing development costs

A company is producing a computer program for a new cash point. The company uses Rapid Application Development (RAD). Describe what is meant by Rapid Application Development (RAD) and how it can be used to help in producing the program. [F452 Q2 Jun 2011 (4)]

- A mock-up/prototype of the program produced ... with reduced functionality
- ...to a set deadline
- It is tested / feedback is obtained from users
- These results are used to inform the next prototype
- The process is repeated (until final, a fully working version is produced)

2

The structure of procedural programs

2.1 DEFINE AND CORRECTLY USE THE FOLLOWING TERMS AS THEY APPLY TO PROCEDURAL PROGRAMMING: STATEMENT, SUBROUTINE, PROCEDURE, FUNCTION, PARAMETER/ARGUMENT, SEQUENCE, SELECTION, ITERATION/REPETITION, LOOP

A *statement* is a single executable line of a program.

A *subroutine* is a section of code within a larger body of code. It performs a specific task and is invoked or 'called' (often many times at many different points) from within the main body of code.

A *procedure* is a subroutine which returns either no values or possibly many.

A *function* is a subroutine which returns a single value.

A *parameter* or *argument* is a variable which holds either a value or an address and is 'passed' to a subroutine where it is given a new identifier in the subroutine. Parameters are normally passed on the stack.

Sequence is the term used to describe the execution of instructions one after the other in the order in which they are written.

Selection is the term used to describe the execution of a instruction or set of instructions depending upon some condition. Typical examples are IF THEN ELSE or SELECT CASE control structures.

Iteration, repetition or *loop* is the repeated execution of an instruction or set of instructions either a set number of times (FOR) loop, WHILE (some condition is true) or REPEAT-UNTIL (some condition is true). A WHILE loop tests the condition at the start of the loop with the result that any instructions inside the loop will not be executed at all if the condition is false when the loop is first entered. A REPEAT-UNTIL loop tests the condition at the end of the loop which means that any instructions inside the body of the loop will be executed at least once.

A computer program consists of many statements which are sometimes organised into subroutines such as functions. Explain what is meant by a statement. [F452 Q5 Jan 2009 (2)]

- A single instruction ... which can be executed

Explain what is meant by a function. (2)

- A subroutine ... which can return a single value

Functions and procedures are both examples of subprograms. Explain how a function differs from a procedure. [F452 Q4 Specimen Questions (2)

- A function returns a single value to the calling program so that it can be used in ... the same way as a variable in the main body of the program
- A procedure can return none or many.

Describe what is meant by a function. [F452 Q2 June 2010 (3)]

- A subroutine/subprogram/module of code
- ... which returns a single value
- It can be called using its identifier
- ... as part of an expression
- The value returned replaces the function call

The design for a computer program contains the following algorithm shown in pseudo-code.

```
01 INPUT A
02 INPUT B
03 C = 0
04 IF A = B THEN
05    B = 1
06 ELSE
07    WHILE B > A
08       B = B - A
09       C = C + 1
10    END WHILE
11    A = B
12 END IF
```

Define the terms Statement and Selection and for each, give an example from the algorithm. [F452 Q3 Jan 2011 (2,2)]

Statement

- A single step/instruction within the algorithm
- Any of the lines would provide a suitable example

Selection

- Whether code is executed depends on a condition
- E.g. IF statement in line(s) 04 (to 12)

A sequence of numbers begins 2, 4, 7, ... Here is an algorithm in pseudo-code for a function which returns the nth number of the sequence. For example, SequenceItem(3) returns the 3rd number in the sequence.

```
01  FUNCTION SequenceItem(n:INTEGER)  :  INTEGER
02    Answer = 1
03    FOR i = 1 TO n
04      Answer = Answer + i
05    NEXT i
06    RETURN Answer
07  END FUNCTION
```

This algorithm uses iteration. Describe what is meant by iteration, and show how it has been used in this algorithm. [F452 Q4 Jun 2011 (4)]

- (A section of) code is executed repeatedly
- ...for a fixed number of times
- ...or until a condition is met
- In the algorithm line 04 is repeated inside the FOR Loop which runs from line 3 to line 5
- ...n times

A program contains the following procedure to calculate the number of tiles needed to cover a floor.

```
01  PROCEDURE solveit(L, W, T)
02  a = L DIV T
03  b = (W DIV T) + 1
04  c = a * b
05  d = c + (c DIV 10)
06  OUTPUT d
07  END PROCEDURE
```

This procedure has parameters. Describe what is meant by a parameter. [F452 Q2 Jan 2010 (3)]

- A variable which holds an item of data ...which is supplied/passed to a subroutine/procedure/function
- It is given an identifier when the subroutine is defined
- It is substituted by an actual value when the subroutine is called

State the parameters of this procedure. (1)

- L, W, T

2.2 IDENTIFY THE THREE BASIC PROGRAMMING CONSTRUCTS USED TO CONTROL EXECUTION, I.E. SEQUENCE, SELECTION AND ITERATION

The previous section defined each of these terms and gave some examples of how they might appear in exam questions. The examiners might very well ask you to produce definitions for each of these terms, but they are also quite likely to ask you to identify these programming constructs in a short piece of code. If the code is linear, i.e. one line after the other then you are dealing with sequence. If you're faced with an 'IF THEN' or 'CASE SELECT' construct then you're clearly dealing with selection and if it's one of the three loop constructs then you're dealing with iteration.

Here are some more examples specifically about one of these three programming constructs.

Programming constructs determine the way in which statements in a program are executed. Three types of programming constructs are sequence, selection and iteration. Describe what is meant by each of these. [F452 Q1 Jun 2009 (2,2,2)]

Sequence

- All instructions are executed
- ...once
- ...in the order in which they appear

Selection

- A condition is used
- ...to determine which of the statements (if any) will be executed
- As a result some instructions may not be executed

Iteration

- A group of instructions is repeated
- ...for a set number of times
- ...or until a condition is met

A computer program contains the following instructions

```
X = 5
Y = 7
X = Y
OUTPUT X
```

State which of the programming constructs have been used. (1)

- Sequence

State the value which will be output. (1)

- 7

2.3   UNDERSTAND AND USE SELECTION IN PSEUDO-CODE AND A PROCEDURAL PROGRAMMING LANGUAGE

Selection in procedural languages is essentially achieved by using IF-THEN or IF-THEN-ELSE constructs. A simple IF-THEN construct might be the following.

```
IF (X < 0) THEN
   PRINT 'X is negative'
ENDIF
```

If in addition we wanted to tell the user when X was positive we might write

```
IF (X < 0) THEN
  PRINT 'X is negative'
ENDIF
IF (X >= 0) THEN
  PRINT 'X is positive'
ENDIF
```

Clearly this would be expressed more simply if we used the construct IF-THEN-ELSE as shown in the following fragment.

```
IF (X < 0) THEN
  PRINT 'X is negative'
ELSE
  PRINT 'X is positive'
ENDIF
```

If X were zero we might want to tell the user this as well, so we might write the following

```
IF (X < 0) THEN
  PRINT 'X is negative'
ELSE
  IF (X = 0) THEN
    PRINT 'X is zero'
  ELSE
    PRINT 'X is positive'
  ENDIF
ENDIF
```

Questions from this part of the specification often ask you to create your own IF-THEN statements in response to a given situation. These are usually very straightforward and you may need to use logical operators such as AND and OR as in the following example.

Wayne is writing an application for a touch screen mobile phone to identify types of ladybird. Wayne uses IF statements in the code to determine whether the data input matches known types of ladybird. Wayne uses the following IF statement to determine whether the spot colour which has been input matches a type of ladybird which has white spots.

```
IF InputSpotColour = 'WHITE' THEN
```

Show how an IF statement can be used to check whether the spot colour which has been input matches a ladybird which can have either red or black spots. [F452 Q1 Jun 2011 (2)]

The correct answer is

```
IF (InputSpotColour = Black) OR (InputSpotColour = Red)
```

and marks were awarded as follows

- Testing for black/red
- For correct use of OR

Wayne's program uses the following variables.
- **InputSpots: The number of spots input by the user.**
- **MaxSpots, MinSpots: The maximum and minimum number of spots that a type of ladybird can have.**

Show how an IF statement can be used to check whether the value of InputSpots is within the range from MinSpots to MaxSpots. (3)

The correct answer is

```
IF (MinSpots <= InputSpots) AND (InputSpots <= MaxSpots) THEN
```

and marks were awarded for

- MinSpots <= InputSpots
- AND
- InputSpots <= MaxSpots

Wayne's program also contains the following variables.
- **InputLength: The length input by the user.**
- **AveLength: The average length of a type of ladybird.**

Show how an IF statement can be used to check whether the value of InputLength is within 1mm of AveLength. (3)

The correct answer is

```
IF (InputLength >= AveLength-1) AND (InputLength <= AveLength+1) THEN
```

Marks were awarded as follows

- Matches if InputLength = AveLength
- Matches if InputLength = AveLength+1 or AveLength-1 (i.e. boundaries of range)
- Does not match for any values outside range

It is essential when using more than one IF-THEN construct as in first example in this section, that code is indented otherwise it can be pretty impossible to work out what is going on. IF-THEN-ELSE constructs are fine in small doses, but if you were writing a game where a character can move as in the next question, a SELECT-CASE construct is much cleaner.

A company produces a game which is to be played on mobile phones. In the game, a character moves forward and backward along a platform, and can also jump or duck to avoid obstacles. The game is controlled using the standard keypad of the telephone.

The pseudo-code to control the character is

```
01 REPEAT
02   INPUT Key
03   Move Character according to the key input
04 UNTIL the end of platform is reached
```

To implement line 03 of the pseudo-code, the programmers decide to use a SELECT CASE statement. Explain what is meant by a SELECT CASE statement, and how it can be used to move the character. [F452 Q3 Jan 2010 (4)]

- The value of a variable/expression is used
- ...to decide which of a number of statement blocks is executed
- There can be a default option
- In this case, different code blocks for different moves (jump, duck, forward, backward)
- ...will be executed depending on the value of the key input
- ...or a sensible response (e.g. beep) if a wrong key is pressed

Answers to this question could also have been accepted in pseudo-code, an example of which might have been the following (assuming the character is moving left to right).

```
SELECT CASE of Key
'2' : Character jumps
'4' : Character moves backward
'6' : Character moves forward
'8' : Character ducks
Default : Beep!
END CASE
```

The same code written as a series of IF-THEN-ELSE constructs might have been written as

```
IF Key = '2' THEN
  Character jumps
ELSE
  IF Key = '4'
    Character moves backward
  ELSE
    IF Key = '6'
      Character moves forward
    ELSE
      IF Key = '8'
        Character ducks
      ELSE
        Beep!
      ENDIF
    ENDIF
  ENDIF
ENDIF
```

Clearly not as clean and easy to understand as the SELECT-CASE version.

2.4 UNDERSTAND AND USE ITERATION IN PSEUDO-CODE AND A PROCEDURAL PROGRAMMING LANGUAGE

As discussed on page 25 there are essentially three forms of iteration in procedural programming languages. The first, FOR-NEXT loops create an iteration which occurs a fixed number of times (though it is always possible to break out of the loop earlier if necessary). A typical FOR-NEXT loop in pseudo-code which printed the first ten numbers together with their square and cube might be as follows.

```
01 FOR X = 1 UNTIL 10
02    PRINT X, X*X, X*X*X
03 NEXT I
```

WHILE-ENDWHILE loops iterate while a condition tested at the beginning of the loop remains true. This means that if the condition was false on entry to the loop, the code inside the loop will not get executed at all. A typical WHILE-ENDWHILE construct, again in pseudo-code might be as follows. Note that its purpose is the same as the previous example, i.e. to print the first ten numbers together with their square and cube.

```
01 X = 1
02 WHILE (X <= 10)
03    PRINT X, X*X, X*X*X
04    X = X + 1
05 ENDWHILE
```

REPEAT-UNTIL loops iterate while a condition tested at the end of the loop remains true. This means that they will always run through the code in the loop at least once. A REPEAT-UNTIL version of the previous two loops is as follows.

```
01 X = 1
02 REPEAT
03    PRINT X, X*X, X*X*X
04    X = X + 1
05 UNTIL (X > 10)
```

As in the three simple examples above, it is always possible to re-write any of the three loop constructs in either of the other two forms. It is perfectly possible that the examiner might ask you to do this. The only problem you are likely to have is ensuring that the stopping condition (i.e. the condition that ends the loop) is correct. Note that the WHILE-ENDWHILE loop continues whilst the condition (X<=10) remains true. The corresponding REPEAT-UNTIL loop runs until the condition (X>10) is true. I.e. it will repeat whilst (X>10) is false, or in other words whilst (X<=10) is true, at which point it will terminate. The logic is the same.

Returning to the previous question of moving a character in a mobile phone game, the code of which is shown again.

```
01 REPEAT
02    INPUT Key
03    Move Character according to the key input
04 UNTIL the end of platform is reached
```

This code uses iteration. Describe what is meant by iteration. [F452 Q3 Jan 2010 (2)]

- A (group of) statement(s) executed repeatedly
- …until a condition is met
- …or for a set number of times

Describe two types of iteration construct other than the type used in the pseudo-code above. (4)

WHILE loop

- …The condition is tested before each iteration
- …and the statements in the loop will be executed if the condition is true

- The statements in the loop may not be executed (if the condition is initially false)

FOR loop

- …The number of iterations is fixed
- …according to start and end values of a variable set at the beginning

You may be asked to convert one loop construct into another as in the following example.

The following algorithm for a function CheckTotalLength() contains a FOR loop in lines 03 to 05. Rewrite this FOR loop as a WHILE loop. [F452 Q2 Jun 2010 (5)]

```
01 FUNCTION CheckTotalLength() : BOOLEAN
02    TotalLength = 0
03    FOR i = 1 TO NumberOfSongs
04       TotalLength = TotalLength +  SongLength(i)
05    NEXT i
06    RETURN (TotalLength > 80)
07 END FUNCTION
```

A correct answer would be

```
i=1
WHILE i <= NumberOfSongs
   TotalLength = TotalLength + SongLength(i)
   i=i+1
END WHILE
```

Other solutions are possible and the examiners awarded marks according to the following criteria

- i initialised correctly (typically 1 or 0)
- A WHILE loop has been used correctly
- …and the condition of the while loop (and the initial value of i) ensure that the correct number of iterations are made
- Songlength(i) is added to the TotalLength within each iteration
- The value of i is incremented (or decremented, as appropriate) within each iteration

2.5 UNDERSTAND AND USE NESTED SELECTION AND ITERATION STATEMENTS

Describe what is meant by nesting. [F452 Q1 Jun 2011 (2)]

- When one construct is written within another
- Each construct must be completely contained in the preceding construct/they are not allowed to overlap
- Correct example

The design for a game contains the following pseudo-code

```
01 IF Character has reached end of platform
02    Display ''YOU WIN''
03    REPEAT
04       Play Music
```

```
05 END IF
06    UNTIL any key is pressed
```

Explain why this pseudo-code contains an error. [F452 Q3 Jan 2010 (2)]

- The IF statement and the REPEAT loop are nested incorrectly (mark for correct use of the term)
- The REPEAT Loop should be completely within the IF statement
- Lines 05 and 06 are the wrong way round
- As it is, the REPEAT inside the IF has no UNTIL/ the ENDIF inside the REPEAT has no IF

State the type of error the pseudo-code contains and when the error would be detected if implemented. (2)

- Syntax (error)
- When the program is translated

The design for a computer program contains the following algorithm shown in pseudo-code.

```
01 INPUT A
02 INPUT B
03 C = 0
04 IF A = B THEN
05    B = 1
06 ELSE
07    WHILE B > A
08       B = B - A
09       C = C + 1
10    END WHILE
11    A = B
12 END IF
```

Explain how nesting has been used in the algorithm above. You should refer to line numbers in your answer. [F452 Q3 Jan 2011 (3)]

- While is contained within the IF Statement
- …as the IF statement goes from 04(06) to 12
- …and the WHILE statement goes from 07 to 10

2.6   UNDERSTAND, CREATE AND USE SUBROUTINES

This section tests how well you can read and understand functions and procedures when parameters are passed to them.

To calculate the fare in a program calculating the cost of a bus journey, the program uses the following function.

```
01 FUNCTION CalculateFare(Start, Destination, Type)
02    CONSTANT PensionerMax = 0.50
03    Distance = Destination - Start
04    Fare = Distance * 0.20
```

```
05    IF Type =  CHILD  THEN
06       Fare = Fare / 2
07    END IF
08    IF Type =  PENSIONER  AND Fare > PensionerMax
09       Fare = PensionerMax
10    END IF
11    RETURN Fare
12 END FUNCTION
```

Use the function to calculate the fare for the following journeys. You must show your working. [F452 Q1 Jan 2011 (3,4,4)]

Start = 1, Destination = 4, Type = ADULT

- Distance = 4 - 1 so Distance = 3
- Fare = 3 * 0.20
- All IF statements are False and not executed
- 0.60 is returned

Start = 5, Destination = 6, Type = CHILD

- Distance = 6 - 5 so Distance = 1
- Fare = 1 * 0.20
- As Type = CHILD is TRUE
- ...Fare = 0.20/2
- 0.10 is returned

Start = 2, Destination = 5, Type = PENSIONER

- Distance = 5 - 2 so Distance = 3
- Fare = 3 * 0.20 = 0.60
- As Type = PENSIONER AND Fare > PensionerMax are both TRUE
- ...Fare = PensionerMax
- 0.50 is returned

A company is producing a computer program for a new cash point. Here is part of the code for the program. This code contains some errors.

```
01 PROCEDURE WithdrawCash(AccountNo:INTEGER)
02    VARIABLE Amount:REAL //how much to withdraw
03    VARIABLE Print:BOOLEAN //whether a receipt is wanted
04    Amount = GetAmountWanted()
05    Print = GetWhetherReceiptWanted()
06    IF Balance(AccountNo) < Amount THEN
07       DispenseCash(Amount)
08       IF Print = TRUE THEN
09          PrintReceipt(AccountNo, Amount)
10       END IF
11    ELSE
12       OUTPUT ''Insufficient Funds''
13    END IF
14 END PROCEDURE
```

In this extract the procedure WithdrawCash is defined. Define the term procedure and explain how a procedure is used. [F452 Q2 Jun 2011 (4)]

- A subroutine/subprogram / Section of code which is given an identifier
- It can be called from the main program / from another procedure
- When called the code in the procedure is executed
- And then control is passed back to where the procedure is called

State the name of a procedure used in the code other than WithdrawCash. (1)

- DispenseCash/PrintReceipt

GetAmountWanted is a function which prompts the user for an amount to withdraw and returns this amount. Explain one difference between a procedure and a function. (2)

- A function returns a single value (Accept void functions, i.e. functions that return nothing)
- A procedure does not return a value/returns values by reference

Or alternatively

- A function is used as part of an expression
- A procedure is used as an instruction/statement

State the name of a function used in the code other than GetAmountWanted. (1)

- GetWhetherReceiptWanted/Balance/GetAmountWanted

Explain what is meant by a parameter, using an example from the code. (3)

- (A description of an item of) data which is given to a procedure/ function
- ...it is given a variable/name when procedure is defined
- Example: AccountNo (is a parameter of WithdrawCash)/Amount (on line 7) / AccountNo (on line 9) / Amount (on line 9)

A coin-operated vending machine has 2 slots. Slot A is for 10p coins, and slot B is for 5p coins.

The software of the machine has a function called CoinValue which takes a single character "A" or "B" and returns the value of a coin which has dropped in that slot as an integer. Any other character will produce an error.

State the result of evaluating each of the following expressions. [F452 Q5 Jan 2009 (1,1,1)]

CoinValue("A")

- 10 (Slot A is used for 10p coins)

CoinValue("B") = 5

- TRUE (Slot B is used for 5p coins so this statement is true)

CoinValue("AA")

- Error (The machine takes single characters only)

2.7   IDENTIFY AND USE RECURSION TO SOLVE PROBLEMS

Recursion is an important concept in computer science and a large number of problems are most naturally solved in a recursive manner. One of the simplest and most cited example of recursion is that of producing the factorial of a given number. For those who have not met the factorial notation, an exclamation mark written directly after a number such as 5! is a short-hand for the product of all numbers starting from 1 up to and including the number itself. So for example, 3! = $3 \times 2 \times 1$ = 6 and 5! = $5 \times 4 \times 3 \times 2 \times 1$ = 120. Factorials grow very quickly so for example 10! = $3, 628, 800$ whilst 20! = $2, 432, 902, 008, 176, 640, 000$. Calculators give up pretty quickly.

So, why use recursion to work out factorials?

Consider. 4! = $4 \times 3 \times 2 \times 1$ but $3 \times 2 \times 1$ = 3! so 4! = $4 \times 3!$. Similarly, 3! = $3 \times 2!$ and 2! = $2 \times 1!$ and by definition 1! = 1. Generally, $n! = n \times (n-1)!$. We can use this fact to compute the factorial of a number n very simply as the following function shows.

```
01 FUNCTION factorial(n : integer) : integer
02    IF n = 1
03       return 1
04    ELSE
05       return n x factorial(n-1)
06 END FUNCTION
```

Let's trace what happens when we call factorial with $n = 3$.

On line 02, n isn't 1 so we jump to line 04, then line 05 where eventually we will return 3 x factorial(2) to the line where we were originally called. We call our function again, this time with $n = 2$.

On line 02, n isn't 1 so we jump to line 04, then line 05 where we will return 2 x factorial(1) to where we were called, i.e. line 05. We call our function again, this time with $n = 1$.

This time, on line 02, n is 1 so we return the value 1 to the point where we were called, i.e. line 05. We now return $2 \times 1 = 2$ to the point at which we were were called earlier, i.e. again line 05 where we finally return from the function itself with the value $3 \times 2 = 6$.

State what is meant by recursion [F452 Q5 Jan 2009 (1)]

- When a function/procedure/subroutine calls itself

Every algorithm which uses iteration can also be written using recursion. Describe what is meant by a recursive algorithm. [F452 Q4 Jun 2011 (2)]

- A subroutine/function/procedure
- ...calls itself
- Until it reaches a base case

A sequence of numbers begins 2, 4, 7, ... Here is an algorithm in pseudo-code for a function which returns the nth number of the sequence. For example, SequenceItem(3) returns the 3rd number in the sequence.

```
01 FUNCTION SequenceItem(n:INTEGER) : INTEGER
02    Answer = 1
03    FOR i = 1 TO n
04      Answer = Answer + i
05    NEXT i
06    RETURN Answer
07 END FUNCTION
```

Write a recursive function in a high level language of your choice to find the nth number in the sequence. State the name of the language you use. Use good program writing techniques to ensure that your code can be understood by another programmer. (7)

The answer is very similar to that of finding the factorial of a number, but in this case we need to add rather than multiply as we go along but noting that SequenceItem(1) = 2.

```
// Function to compute sequence 2, 4, 7 ... using recursion
// Sequence is generated for integer n using the formula
// n = n + (n-1) + (n-2) + ... 2 + 1 + 1
FUNCTION SequenceItem(n:INTEGER) : INTEGER
  IF n = 1 THEN
    RETURN 2 // return 2 for the first number in the sequence
  ELSE // otherwise, add n to the previous number
    RETURN n + SequenceItem(n-1)
  END IF
END FUNCTION
```

Good programming techniques are shown by writing comments where appropriate, indenting and using sensible variable names (not relevant in this particular example).

2.8 SHOW AN UNDERSTANDING OF THE STRUCTURE OF A RECURSIVE SUBROUTINE, INCLUDING THE NECESSITY OF A STOPPING CONDITION

Recursive functions can be excellent solutions to many types of problems, but care must always be taken to ensure that a *stopping condition* is in place. A stopping condition is a condition under which the recursive function stops recursing and returns to the point where it had been called. In the previous example and that of the factorial function, the stopping condition is met when n=1. When any function is called, the return address and any parameters are passed on the stack. Recursive functions that call themselves without a stopping condition will cause the stack to grow until there is no more memory available and the program will simply crash. In recursive functions with a stopping condition but one which is possibly not called for a long time as in the case of calling the previous function with say a value of 1,000,000, it is perfectly possible that the program will run out of stack space before managing to reach the stopping condition.

An application contains the following function.

```
01 FUNCTION Mystery(n : Integer) : Integer
02    IF n < 10 THEN
03      RETURN n
04    ELSE
05      RETURN Mystery (n - 9)
```

```
06   END IF
07 END FUNCTION
```

Using this example, explain what is meant by a recursive function. [F452 Q4 Jun 2010 (3)]

- A function which calls itself
- The original call is halted
- ...until subsequent calls return
- Eventually reaches a stopping condition
- For example the function mystery calls itself in line 05
- ...and the recursion will stop when $n < 10$

State the value which will be returned by Mystery(5) and justify your answer.

- Value returned : 5

Justification:

- $n = 5$
- On line 02 the condition of the IF statement is TRUE/n(5) is less than 10
- So on line 03, the value of n (which is 5) will be returned

2.9   TRACE THE EXECUTION OF A RECURSIVE SUBROUTINE INCLUDING CALLS TO ITSELF

A typical question on recursion will often ask you to trace through a recursive function as in this next example.

Trace the execution of the call Mystery(15) in the example above, showing every function call and the value returned. [F452 Q4 Jun 2010 (5)]

- Call Mystery(15). i.e. where n = 15
- Line 02 ...condition is FALSE
- RETURN Mystery(15 - 9) (in line 05)
- ...New call to Mystery(6). i.e. n = 6
- ......Line 02 is TRUE
- ......Return 6 to Mystery (15 - 9) (in line 05 of previous call)
- Final return value is 6

A coin-operated vending machine has 2 slots. Slot A is for 10p coins, and slot B is for 5p coins. The software of the machine has a function called CoinValue which takes a single character "A" or "B" and returns the value of a coin which has dropped in that slot as an integer. Any other character will produce an error.

The machine records the coins that have been entered using a string of the characters A and B. (So "ABB" means that a 10p coin was entered followed by two 5p coins.) The software in the machine uses the following recursive function.

```
01 BEGIN Function Calculate(CoinString)
02    IF Length of CoinString = 1 THEN
03       Calculate = CoinValue(CoinString)
04    ELSE
```

```
05        First = First Character in CoinString
06        Rest = All the characters in CoinString after the first
07        Calculate = CoinValue(First) + Calculate(Rest)
08     END IF
09 END Function
```

State the result of the function if it is called with the following arguments. [F452 Q5 Jan 09 (1,1)]

Calculate("AA")

- 20

Calculate("BABAA")

- 40

The function Calculate is called with the argument "AB". Trace the execution of Calculate("AB") indicating clearly
- **each time the function is called**
- **the value of the argument in each call**
- **the lines of the algorithm that are executed**
- **the value that is returned from each function call.**
You may use a diagram in your answer.

- Function called with argument ("AB")
- Line 02 IF statement is false so do lines 04,05,06
- Line 07 Coinvalue(A) = 10
- Line 07 needs Calculate ("B") so makes a new call
- Function called with argument ("B")
- Line 02 IF Statement is TRUE so do line 03
- Line 03 Calculate = CoinValue("B") = 5
- Line 03 Call ends returning 5
- Line 07 continues: Return value = 10 + 5 = 15
- Call ends returning 15

2.10   DISCUSS THE RELATIVE MERITS OF ITERATIVE AND RECURSIVE SOLUTIONS TO THE SAME PROBLEM

The function Mystery() can be written using iteration instead of recursion, as shown below.

```
FUNCTION Mystery(n : INTEGER) : INTEGER
  Temp = n
  WHILE Temp > _____
    Temp = Temp - 9
  END WHILE
  RETURN _____
END FUNCTION
```

Fill in the blank spaces in the algorithm above. [F452 Q4 Jun 2010 (2)]

```
FUNCTION Mystery(n : INTEGER) : INTEGER
   Temp = n
   WHILE Temp > 9 (will also accept >= 10)
     Temp = Temp - 9
   END WHILE
   RETURN Temp
END FUNCTION
```

Explain ONE advantage and ONE disadvantage of using iteration instead of recursion when writing functions. (2,2)

Advantage

- Uses only one set of variables (which are updated on each loop)/ recursion creates new variables for each call
- ...therefore more efficient use of memory ...
- ...and can be faster ...
- ...less likely to run out of stack space...

Disadvantage

- Algorithm may be more difficult to follow/trace ...
- ...because variables are being reused
- You need to be careful to get the conditions of loops correct (given current state of variables)
- Humans often express the problem in a recursive way

Data types and data structures

3.1 Define different data types, e.g. numeric (integer, real), Boolean, character and string

Programs use data. Data comes in various *types*.

There are *integers*, i.e. whole numbers in some range, Integers are usually represented by 32 bits and 2^{32} = 4,294,967,296 which, split evenly between positive and negative numbers give us the range -2,147,483,648 — 2,147,483,647.

There are *real* numbers, often called *floats*, short for floating point. The examiners will expect you to say that they are represented in the computer with either 4 or 8 bytes and are structured in such a fashion that they can represent numbers with decimal points, for example, 1,237.5312 or -1,350.25.

Programs invariably need some representation of whether a statement is true or false and *booleans* do this. They are normally one byte long and represent either TRUE or FALSE or alternatively, YES or NO.

A *char* is one byte long and holds the ASCII value of a character such as a letter 'A' or 'ε'.

A *string* is a one dimensional array of characters and requires the same amount of space in bytes as there are characters in the string. For example the string "This is a banana sandwich" has 25 characters and will typically take up 25 bytes of storage.

You might be asked to estimate the storage for a *date*. Dates are usually in the form "xx/xx/xxxx" such as "11/07/2011". Ignoring the '/' characters, this can be represented by 8 bytes.

A function CheckTotalLength() returns a value of data type Boolean. State what is meant by a Boolean data type. [F452 Q2 Jun 2010 (1)]

- A data type which can accept only two values/(e.g.) TRUE or FALSE

3.2 Select and use them appropriately in their solutions to problems

To take part in a mobile phone quiz, players must register their 11 digit mobile phone number (with no spaces or other characters). Explain why the phone number should not be stored as an integer. [F452 Q3 Jun 2011 (2)]

- A phone number is not a value
- ...but a sequence of digits / a string
- Phone numbers may have leading zeros
- ...which would be lost if stored as an integer

Some variables used in a program are given below. For each variable, state its data type and give one reason why this data type is suitable. [F452 Q4 Jun 2009 (2,2,2,2)]

Variable: NoTickets (The number of tickets wanted)

- Integer
- Only whole numbers of tickets can be ordered

Variable: SeatAvailable (Whether a seat can be booked)

- Boolean
- There are only two possible values (yes-no/true-false etc)

Variable: SeatNumber (For example F7, meaning the seat is in row F, number 7)

- String
- The value contains letters as well as digits

Variable: TotalPrice (The cost of the tickets booked by the customer)

- Currency/real
- The values will include decimal fractions/to allow for pence

3.3 Define and use arrays

An array is a set of data of the same type grouped together using the same identifier. Each of the data items in an array is addressed by the variable name and a *subscript* or *index*. For example suppose you want keep track of 100 scores in a game. Each score can be represented by an integer. One hundred scores could be held in the array scores[100]. The exact syntax of how an array is declared is dependent on what language you're using. In C or C++ you'd write "int scores[100]", in Pascal you'd write "var scores:array[1..100] of integer", in Java "int[] scores = new int[100]" and in Visual Basic "Dim scores(1 to 100) as integer". In each case the statement reserves space for 100 integers.

You are not restricted to one dimensional arrays. If you were writing a board game such as tic-tac-toe (noughts and crosses), you'd want to keep track of a board that is of size 3 x 3. To do so, you would need to create a two dimensional array using syntax like "int board[3][3]" in C or C++ and in Java, "int[][] board = new int[3][3]".

The above statements create (or *declare*)arrays. You will also want to *initialise* an array. If it's a simple one dimensional array to set 100 integers to zero, a simple piece of pseudo-code might be.

```
for i = 1 to 100
  ourArray[i] = 0
next i
```

To initialise a 3 x 3 two dimensional array, you'd simply need a second loop as in

```
for i = 1 to 3
  for j = 1 to 3
    board[i][j] = 0
  next j
next i
```

Let's suppose that you're searching a one-dimensional array called names, holding 100 strings for the name John. You might do this using the pseudo-code

```
boolean found = FALSE;
for i = 1 to 100
  if names[i] = ''John''
    found = TRUE
next i
if found
  then print ''We found him!''
else
  print ''We didn't find him''
```

In this short piece of pseudo-code we create a boolean (we usually call this a flag, the Americans call it a semaphore) to hold the result of our search for John. We start out by assuming that we haven't found him. We then iterate through the loop. If we find the name 'John', we set the flag to TRUE. If we've run through all 100 names and we've still not found him,the flag will still be FALSE. We can then put up an appropriate message.

A television talent contest allows the audience to vote for one of three contestants, A, B or C, using a voting pad. An early version of the software assumes that there are 100 people in the audience. To store their votes, it uses an array of 100 characters. Describe one advantage of using an array rather than 100 separate variables in this implementation. [F452 Q3 Specimen Questions (2)]

- Code is easier to manage
- ...as there are fewer variables
- Can use iteration (to count up the votes)/looping
- ...instead of dealing with each vote separately
- Code will be more easily scaleable/they can easily change the number of voters
- ...by changing the size of the array

Give two items which need to be stated when defining an array, giving one reason for each item. (4)

- Name of array
- ...to allow individual data items to be accessed
- Maximum number of elements/size of array/bounds of array

- ...to enable contiguous locations in memory to be reserved
- Data type of contents
- ...to allow correct variables/to determine rules for manipulation
- Dimension
- ...to allow position in array to have meaning

By referring to this example or otherwise, explain why it is necessary to initialise arrays before using them. (2)

- It is good practice to always initialise arrays before using them otherwise the array may start with spurious values
- ...that we might later rely on
- In the case of this example we would clearly want all array elements to start at zero

The Anytown Bus Company uses a computer program to calculate the bus fares of journeys and to print bus tickets. The program uses an array called BusStop to store the names of all the stops in the order of travel. The beginning of the array for a particular route is shown below.

High Street
Station Road
Green Lane
Avenue
New Street
Kingsway

The value of BusStop(1) is High Street. State the value of BusStop(4). [F452 Q1 Jan 2011 (1)]

- Avenue

When the program is used, the driver enters the name of a stop. The program needs a function which will return the position of that stop in the array BusStop. State the position which should be returned if the name entered is Kingsway. (1)

- 6

Describe how a serial search can be used to determine the position when a name held in an array is entered. (5)

- Check the array is not empty (and report an error if it is)
- Set a counter to 1/0/start from first position
- Check if item (at current position) is item searched
- If found return the position/value of counter
- If not found increment counter/move to next position
- Until the end of the array / until item found
- If item still not found, return Not Found

A printing company uses a computer program to randomly generate and print bingo tickets. Each bingo ticket has a grid with three rows and nine columns. Each row contains 5 numbers and 4 blank spaces.

4			32	45		68		82
9		26			51	62		88
		24		47	55	65	71	

The computer program stores the numbers in a 2-dimensional array called Ticket. Explain what is meant by an array. [F452 Q3 Jun 2010 (3)]

- A data structure/contains several data items
- ...of the same data type
- ...grouped under one identifier
- Individual items are accessed using an index
- Stored contiguously in computer memory

State THREE items which should be specified when declaring an array. (3)

- Identifier/name
- Data type
- Dimensions (i.e. 1D, 2D etc..)
- Size of the array/upper and lower bounds

In the array Ticket, the first index represents the row and the second represents the column.
e.g. Ticket(1,4) = 32 means the number on row 1, column 4 is 32.
To generate the tickets, the computer program first fills in the columns with random integers as specified in the table below.

Column	Highest Possible Random Integer	Lowest Possible Random Integer
1	10	1
2	20	11
3	30	21
4	40	31
5	50	41
6	60	51
7	70	61
8	80	71
9	90	81

The algorithm used to fill the array with random numbers is given below. Complete this algorithm by filling in the spaces. (4)

```
01 For Column = 1 to _____
02   Highest = Column * _____
03   Lowest = _____ - 9
04   For Row = 1 to _____
05     Ticket(Row,Column) = Random integer between Highest and Lowest
06   Next Row
07 Next Column
```

Answer

- 9 (there are 9 possible numbers for column)
- 10 (the number in the second column is 10*column)
- Highest OR Column * 10
- 3 (three possible values for row)

Examiners often use a single question to cover a range of topics in the syllabus. The following question covers defining an array, analysing an array and finally writing a subroutine in your preferred language to make use of an array.

A company is writing a program to control the lift in a 5-storey building. The program uses an array called LiftCalled( ) to store whether the lift has been called on each floor. Explain what is meant by an array. [F452 Q3 Jun 2009 (2)]

- A data structure / set of data items
- Of the same data type
- Grouped under one identifier
- Each item can be addressed using its index/subscript

The structure of the array used is shown in the table below. Each row represents a floor of the building. The first column stores whether a lift is wanted to go UP from that floor, and the second column stores whether the lift is wanted to go DOWN from that floor.

	1(UP)	2(DOWN)	
1	FALSE	FALSE	
2	TRUE	FALSE	
3	TRUE	FALSE	
4	FALSE	(TRUE)	← LiftCalled(4,2)
5	FALSE	FALSE	

In the table above the value of LiftCalled(4,2) is TRUE. This means that the lift has been called to go DOWN from the fourth floor. State the value of LiftCalled(2,1) and explain what it means. (3)

- Value: TRUE
- Meaning: Called to go UP from the second floor

When the lift is called from a floor (by pressing either UP or DOWN outside the lift door) the program executes a subroutine ButtonPressed. This subroutine updates the contents of the array LiftCalled by inserting TRUE in the cell which corresponds to the floor on which the lift is called and the direction wanted. The algorithm for this subroutine is given below in pseudocode.

```
SubRoutine ButtonPressed (Floor:Integer,Direction:String)
   IF Direction = 'UP' THEN
      LiftCalled(Floor, .....) = TRUE
   ELSE
      LiftCalled(..... , 2 ) = .........
   END IF
End SubRoutine ButtonPressed
```

Fill in the three spaces in the algorithm. (3)

- 1
- Floor
- TRUE

State the names of the parameters of the subroutine. (2)

- Floor
- Direction

Supervisors can call the lift using an override facility. This uses a subroutine call SupervisorCall. This subroutine has one parameter, Floor (the number of the floor where the supervisor is.) The subroutine sets the UP and DOWN values for the designated floor to TRUE, and all other values in the array to FALSE. Write the code for the subroutine SupervisorCall in a high level language. You should state the name of the language you have used and use good program writing techniques to ensure that your code can be understood by another programmer. (6)

The examiners provided the following pseudo-code example.

```
Sub SupervisorCall(Floor : Integer)
   dim iFloor As Integer
   dim iDirection As Integer
   FOR iFloor = 1 to 5
     FOR iDirection = 1 to 2
       IF  iFloor = Floor
         LiftCalled(iFloor, iDirection) = TRUE
       ELSE
         LiftCalled(iFloor, iDirection) = FALSE
       END IF
     NEXT iDirection
   NEXT iFloor
END SUB
```

Marks were awarded for the following points.

- Using "SupervisorCall" as identifier of subroutine
- Using one parameter called Floor (of data type Integer)
- Setting all values of array LiftCalled to False
- ...except for LiftCalled(Floor, 1) and LiftCalled(Floor,2) which are set to TRUE
- Correct use of indentation
- Code annotated / can be understood easily without comments
- Descriptive identifier names

3.4 EXPLAIN THE ADVANTAGES AND DISADVANTAGES OF DIFFERENT DATA TYPES AND DATA STRUCTURES FOR SOLVING A GIVEN PROBLEM

In this section of the specification the examiner is testing whether you are able to assign data types to situations correctly. This is discussed in some detail on page 54, but in summary, use the data type *integer* for whole numbers and *float* or *real* for numbers with decimal points or money. Use *string* or preferably *date* for dates and *boolean* for yes/no or true/false. Use *string* for names, addresses and anywhere you may have both characters and numbers. Finally, use *char* if you need to hold a single character, for example if you need to record 'M' or 'F' for Male or Female.

The Anytown Bus Company uses a computer program to calculate the bus fares of journeys and to print bus tickets. The program uses variables to store the following data. For each variable, state the most suitable data type and give a reason for your choice.

RouteNumber (the number of the bus route. e.g. 65, 5A or N93) [F452 Q1 Jan 2011 (2)]

- String / Text / Alphanumeric
- Consists of a series of characters (some of which happen to be digits) / not a numeric value

Fare (the cost of the journey in pounds e.g. 0.40) (2)

- Real / float / currency
- To allow for pounds and pence

TicketType (the word CHILD, ADULT or PENSIONER) (2)

- String / Text / Alphanumeric
- Consists of a series of characters/ a word

Destination (the position of the destination of the journey in the array BusStop) (2)

- Integer / byte / long
- The position in an array must be a whole number

3.5   DESIGN AND IMPLEMENT A RECORD FORMAT

Implementing a record format is a matter of assigning the correct data types to fields. See the previous section and page 54 for more information on particular types of data items. Examples on this topic can also be found on page 53.

A company organises a mobile phone quiz. To take part, players must register their 11 digit mobile phone number (with no spaces or other characters). As well as the mobile phone number, the file also contains
  • the number of the last question answered correctly
  • whether the player has been eliminated
Design a record format for the file using the table below. [F452 Q3 Jun 2011 (6)]

Field Name	Data Type	Maximum size in bytes
PhoneNumber		
LastCorrectQuestion		
Eliminated		

Answer:

Field Name	Data Type	Maximum size in bytes
PhoneNumber	String / Text / Alphanumeric	11
LastCorrectQuestion	Integer / Byte	1, 2 or 4
Eliminated	Boolean	1

3.6 DEFINE DIFFERENT MODES OF FILE ACCESS: SERIAL, SEQUENTIAL, INDEXED SEQUENTIAL AND RANDOM

Serial files are files in which records are stored in the order in which they were entered. New records are always added at the end of such files. Such files are only searchable by going through the records one by one starting from the beginning and finishing at the end. In a file with 1,000 records, searching for a particular record will involve checking 500 records on average. This isn't terribly efficient or quick.

Sequential files are files in which records are stored according to some key field, perhaps alphabetically. Such files can be searched quickly and efficiently using a simple binary search.

Indexed sequential files are files in which records are stored according to some key field and where one or more indexes have been created to make searching even more efficient. As an example, let us suppose that we have a file of 1,000,000 records where the key field is a surname. Let us further suppose that an alphabetical index has been created so that those whose surname starts with M starts at record 500,000 and those with N at record 560,452. To find someone with surname 'Matthews' the search routine could employ a binary search starting at record 500,000 and ending at record 560,451.

Random files are files in which records have been placed in the file according to some mathematical *hash* algorithm. For example, the algorithm could take the name and address data fields in a student record converting each character to its ASCII code and then generating an address from the combination of codes. This would result in records being scattered across the file. Good hash algorithms minimise this scattering and will avoid 'collisions' where records might overlap. Records in random files can be retrieved very quickly because the search algorithm simply performs the same hash calculation that was performed when storing the record.

Describe what is meant by a serial file. [F452 Q1 Jan 2009 (2)]

- The data is stored chronologically/in the order in which it is entered
- New data always appended / added to the end of the file
- You need to read each preceding item to reach an item you are searching for

State two reasons why a serial file is better than a sequential file for storing data about a food recipe. (2)

- The files are relatively short
- The program will usually need all of the data / unlikely to need to search for individual ingredients
- There is no need to have the ingredients in a particular order

State what is meant by a sequential file. [F452 Q1 Specimen Questions (2)]

- Records are ordered logically
- …according to a (key) field in the record

A 10-pin bowling club uses a computer program to rank its members according to their bowling average. The program uses a file containing records of all the members of the club. Each record contains the following fields about the member:
  - **A member ID consisting of the first letter of their surname followed by 4 digits**
  - **The name of the member**
  - **The date the member joined the club**
  - **The current average score of the member**
  - **The number of games played by the member, since joining.**
The file will be arranged as an indexed sequential file. Using the member file as an example, describe what is meant by an indexed sequential file. [F452 Q1 Jan 2010 4)]

- Records are arranged in order of a primary key
- …which in this case will be MemberID
- An index is kept which is used to jump to groups/blocks of records
- E.g. the index could hold the positions of the first record with letters A, B, C etc.
- The index must be in the same order as the records
- Mention of multiple indices

Explain why an indexed sequential file is a suitable way to organise the member file. (2)

- Given the large number of records
- …accessing a specific record is faster
- …as you do not have to search sequentially from the beginning.

10,000 players register for an online game and their details are held in an indexed sequential file. Define what is meant by an indexed sequential file. [F452 Q3 Jun 2011 (2)]

- Records are stored according to a (unique) key field (e.g. phone number/other suitable example)
- A separate index is kept to allow groups of records to be accessed quickly

Explain why an indexed sequential file is used to store the details of the players. (3)

- Records can be accessed sequentially when all records need to be accessed
- …e.g. when sending questions to all players/ other suitable example
- Records can be accessed quickly when a particular players record is needed
- …e.g. to check if a particular player has sent the right answer / as there is a large number of records

3.7   STORE, RETRIEVE AND SEARCH FOR DATA IN FILES

The examiners expect you to be familiar with storing, retrieving and searching for data in files. To do so competently you will need to be familiar with file access modes, i.e. read, write and append and you will, ideally, have some experience of this using your high level language of choice.

An electronic general knowledge game keeps the 100 highest scores. These are held in a file which contains, for each high score, the following:

- **the name of the player**
- **the score they achieved**
- **the date on which the score was achieved**
- **the average time, in minutes, spent on each question.**

Describe the process for adding a new high score into a file that already contains 100 high scores. The quality of your written communication will be assessed in your answer to this question. [F452 Q1 Specimen Questions (6)]

Points to be made include :

- Open high score file with read access, open new file with write access
- Copy scores from old to new
- …until point of insertion
- Insert score to be entered into new file
- Copy rest of records from the old file
- …except the last which is discarded
- Delete old file/replace old file with new

Or alternatively :

- Load file into memory
- …into an appropriate data structure (such as an array)
- Copy n^{th} entry to position n+1
- …repeated from position 99
- …until point of insertion
- Insert score to be entered
- Save the data from data structure/array back into the file

For further examples of the sort of question that might be asked please refer to section 3.9, page 56.

3.8 Estimate the size of a file from its structure and the number of records

The type of question referred to in this section simply requires you to fill in a table of data items, in each case giving an appropriate data type and the number of bytes this data type will typically take up. You will then need to calculate how many bytes each record will require and given some particular number of records, typically 1,000 or so, how many kilobytes a file storing these records will need. The calculations are pretty straightforward as in the following example.

A 10-pin bowling club uses a computer program to rank its members according to their bowling average. The program uses a file containing records of all the members of the club. Each record contains the following fields about the member.

- **A member ID consisting of the first letter of their surname followed by 4 digits,**
- **The name of the member,**
- **The date the member joined the club,**
- **The current average score of the member,**

- **The number of games played by the member, since joining.**

Using the table below, state the most appropriate data type and size of each field. [F452 Q1 Jan 2010 (10)]

Field	Data Type	Size
MemberID		
Name		
DateJoined		
CurrentAverage		
GamesPlayed		

Answer :

Field	Data Type	Size
MemberID	String / Text / Alphanumeric	5
Name	String / Text / Alphanumeric	10 - 30
DateJoined	Date	2 / 4 / 8
CurrentAverage	Real / Floating Point / Single / Double	4 / 8
GamesPlayed	Integer	2 or 4 or 8

Unique key fields are often numeric - incrementing automatically in many databases. However, in this example you are told that the key field in this instance, i.e. the memberID is made up of the first letter of their surname followed by four digits which means that you're going to need a *String* of length 5 bytes. A person's name is always going to be of type *String*. The examiner also accepts Text or Alphanumeric in this particular example, but String is universally accepted. Names vary in length so the examiners are prepared to accept any number in the range 10 - 30 bytes.

Date is a datatype on its own account so use this whenever you see Date. Date typically takes up 6 or 8 bytes, though here the examiner is prepared to accept 2, 4 or 8.

If one of the fields is an average clearly you're going to need to use a floating point number so *float* or *real* are the sensible choices here. In this particular question *Single* and *Double* are also accepted as they are simply examples of different size floating point numbers. Floating point numbers require either 4 or 8 bytes of storage.

The final field 'GamesPlayed' is clearly a whole number and in such instances, integer is an obvious answer. Less obvious might be *byte* or *unsigned byte* (which both take up 1 byte). Integers are normally 4 bytes long, but can be 2 bytes (in the case of *short* ints) or 8 bytes (in the case of *long* ints).

A field not shown in the example might be 'Sex' where the answer is either 'M' or 'F'. Clearly here, a single character (*char*) would be sufficient. Chars take up a single byte.

In this particular example the examiner might have included the field 'Member Subscription Paid' which is either True or False. This immediately suggests the use of a *boolean* which takes up a single byte.

These questions are usually followed by the examiner asking you to estimate the size of a file based upon the datatypes you have specified for each of the fields. In such cases, simply add the number of bytes from each field to get a total, multiply the total by the number of records (in this case the number of members), multiply the answer by 1.1 (i.e. add 10%) and finally divide by 1024 (preferably, though dividing by 1000 is usually fine). The examiner will have a range within which your answer should fall. These questions are very straightforward and unless you make any arithmetic errors you should get full marks.

The club needs to record details for 2,000 members in the member file. Using your answer to the first part, estimate the size of the file in kilobytes. You must show your working. (5)

- Answers in the first part are added up
- Multiply by 2000 members
- Add 10% (for overheads)
- Divide by 1000 (or preferably 1024) to get kB
- Answer between 45kB and 126kB

A company organises a mobile phone quiz. 10,000 players register and their details are held in an indexed sequential file. To take part, players must register their 11 digit mobile phone number (with no spaces or other characters). As well as the mobile phone number, the file also contains
- **the number of the last question answered correctly**
- **whether the player has been eliminated**

Given the following record format, estimate the size in kilobytes of a file of 10,000 players. You must show your working. [F452 Q3 Jun 2011 (4)]

Field Name	Data Type	Maximum size in bytes
PhoneNumber	String	11
LastCorrectQuestion	Integer	4
Eliminated	Boolean	1

- Answers in the first part are added up (giving 16)
- Multiply by 10,000 members (giving 160,000)
- Add 10% (for overheads) (giving 176,000)
- Divide by 1000 (or preferably 1024) to get 176kB if divided by 1,000, 172kB if divided by 1,024

An electronic general knowledge game keeps track of the 100 highest scores. These are held in a file which contains, for each high score, the following:

- **the name of the player**
- **the score they achieved**
- **the date on which the score was achieved**
- **the average time, in minutes, spent on each question.**

Complete the following table. [F452 Q1 Specimen Questions (8)]

	Data Type	Size of Field
Name		
Score		
Date		
Time		

Answer :

	Data Type	Size of Field
Name	String	10-20
Score	Integer	1/2/4/8
Date	Date (or suitable alternative)	2/4/8
Time	Real	4/8

Estimate the size, in kB, of the file of 100 records, showing your working. (5)

- Record = total of field lengths from table (17 to 44)
- Result multiplied by 100
- 10% overheads added
- Divided by 1024 (or 1000)
- Correct answer calculated. (1.8kB - 4.84kB)

3.9   USE THE FACILITIES OF A PROCEDURAL LANGUAGE TO PERFORM FILE OPERATIONS

A Computing student has written a program which stores and prints recipes. The data entry screen allows the user to enter the following data about each recipe.

- **The name of the recipe (e.g. Sponge Cake)**
- **The number of people the recipe caters for (e.g. 6)**
- **A table of the ingredients of the recipe with 3 columns**

    - **the name of the ingredient (e.g. flour)**
    - **the quantity required (e.g. 300)**
    - **the units in which the quantity required is measured (e.g. grams).**

The student has written the following algorithm for creating the serial file. (In this algorithm a WRITE command writes a string into a text file and moves to the next line.)

```
OPEN OutputFile in Write Mode
WRITE RecipeName to OutputFile
WRITE NumberOfPeople to OutputFile
FOR each ingredient
    WRITE NameOfIngredient,';',Units,';',Quantity to OutputFile
NEXT ingredient
CLOSE OutputFile
```

The student plans to test this algorithm with the following recipe.

Pasta Bake (for 4 people)
Ingredients:
    200 g pasta bows
    500 ml milk
    150 g cheese

Write down how this recipe will be stored in the output file using the algorithm given.
[F452 Q1 Jan 2009 (4)]

Answer :

- Pasta Bake
- 4
- pasta bows;grams;200 milk; ml; 500
- cheese; grams; 150

The program can be used to calculate the quantities necessary to cater for different numbers of people.

- **The user inputs the new number of people**
- **The data for the recipe is read one line at a time**
- **For each ingredient the new quantity is calculated**
- **...and the data is output to a new file**

Write an algorithm for this process. (8)

```
INPUT NewNumberOfPeople
OPEN both files (one for Input/Reading, one for output/writing)
READ a line of text (recipe name) from Input file
WRITE that line to output file
READ a line of text from input
WRITE NewNumberOfPeople to output file / scale number
REPEAT
   READ a line of text from Input
   CALCULATE new recipe quantity
   REPLACE quantity in string
   WRITE string to output file
UNTIL input file gets to end of file
CLOSE all files (which have been opened)
```

Common facilities of procedural languages

4.1 UNDERSTAND AND USE ASSIGNMENT STATEMENTS

All procedural languages have some agreed syntax to allow programmers to assign values to variables. Additionally, all procedural languages have some agreed syntax to allow a programmer to compare values. In most languages these signs are not the same, a notable exception being Visual Basic. Additionally, you will often see pseudo-code treat them as if they are the same.

In Pascal for example the syntax for assignment to use ':=' as in 'A := 10' which assigns the value 10 to the variable A. Comparison in Pascal is the '=' sign as in 'IF (A = B) '.

In languages derived from C (C++, Java, PHP etc.), assignment uses the '=' sign, whilst comparison uses a double equal sign as in 'if (a == b)'. The examiners may well ask you a question to test whether you understand the difference as in the next question.

The design for a computer program contains the following algorithm shown in pseudo-code.

```
01  INPUT A
02  INPUT B
03  C = 0
04  IF A = B THEN
05     B = 1
06  ELSE
07     WHILE B > A
08        B = B  A
09        C = C+ 1
10     END WHILE
11     A = B
12  END IF
```

Explain the difference between the use of A=B on line 4 and line 11, by referring to the type of operation. [F452 Q3 Jan 2011 (4)]

- In line 4 = is a comparison/relational/equality operator
- ...which checks if A is the same as B (and returns TRUE or FALSE)
- In line 11 = is an assignment operator
- ...which sets the value of A to become the value of B

The next question checks that you really do understand what is meant by assignment.

The following algorithm finds the total of all the digits in a number.

```
01 INPUT
02 T = 0
03 WHILE N > 0
04 L = N MOD 10
05 R = N DIV 10
06 T = T + L
07 N = R
08 END WHILE
```

Explain why it would be incorrect to rewrite line 06 as T + L = T. [F452 Q4 Jan 2009 (2)]

- This line is an assignment statement
- The Left Hand Side (LHS) should be a variable / it should be T = T + L
- ...which will take the value of the expression on RHS
- Putting an expression on the LHS will cause a syntax error if the algorithm were implemented

4.2 UNDERSTAND ARITHMETIC OPERATORS INCLUDING OPERATORS FOR INTEGER DIVISION

In addition to assignment and comparison operators, you are expected to be familiar with the standard arithmetic operators such as $+, -, *, /$ and the integer operators modulus (MOD or %) and integer divide (DIV). The modulus is the integer remainder when one integer is divided by another. In languages derived from Pascal and Basic the operator is MOD. Consider the code snippet in the previous section. In line 04, L is assigned the remainder when N is divided by 10. So if N were 17, L would be assigned the value 7. If N were 173, L would be assigned the value 3 and so on. In languages derived from C, the modulus operator is the '%' sign. In which case, line 04 in C would be written as

```
04 L = N % 10
```

Similarly the examiners expect you to be familiar with DIV which refers to the integer division of two numbers. DIV gives you the whole number part of the division. For example, consider line 05 in the previous code snipper which says that R = N DIV 10. If N were 47, R would be assigned the value 4 because 47 DIVided by 10 is 4.7, the whole number part of which is 4. The remainder is captured in the previous line. Most languages do not use DIV but use the familiar division / operator. But care needs to be taken. The result of a division is dependent on the data types of the values involved in the calculation and programmers are often caught out when they expect the result of a calculation to be a float, e.g. 4.713 but instead get an integer, e.g. 4.

4.3 UNDERSTAND A RANGE OF RELATIONAL OPERATORS

Examiners expect you to be familiar with the various relational operators such as $=, <, <=, >, >=$ and $<>$ and to use these to construct expressions. These should have become very familiar to you in your programming classes, but for the sake of completeness.

Determine whether two values are equal	= or ==
Determine whether two values are unequal	<> or !=
Determine whether one value is less than another	<
Determine whether one value is greater than another	>
Determine whether one value is less than or equal to another	<=
Determine whether one value is greater than or equal to another	>=

4.4 UNDERSTAND THE BOOLEAN OPERATORS AND, OR AND NOT AND USE THESE TO CONSTRUCT EXPRESSIONS

All procedural programs use Sequence, Selection and Iteration as their three principal programming constructs. Selection as we saw in section 2.2 on page 27, allows the programmer to make decisions based upon the truth or falsity of some condition. Conditions are often more complex than a simple IF (A=B) THEN construct. Conditions often make use of the Boolean operators AND, OR and NOT to construct expressions. The following tables give the definitions of each of these operators).

x	NOT x
false	true
true	false

x	y	x AND y
false	false	false
false	true	false
true	false	false
true	true	true

x	y	x OR y
false	false	false
false	true	true
true	false	true
true	true	true

Note that NOT simply inverts true and false. AND is only true if *both* x and y are true while OR is true if *either* x or y or both are true. Also note, that in languages derived from C, NOT is represented by '!', AND by '&&' and OR by ||.

Consider the following question.

A computer program is used to monitor a printer and display its status via an LCD display in the front panel. The program includes the following algorithm.

```
01 IF NOT(PaperTrayEmpty) AND (FilesWaiting > 0) THEN
02    OUTPUT 'PRINTING...'
03 ELSE
04    OUTPUT 'PLEASE ADD PAPER'
05 END IF
```

The algorithm is tested when the values of the variables are PaperTrayEmpty = TRUE, FilesWaiting = 3 [F452 Q3 Jan 2009 (1,1,1,1)]

State the value of NOT(PaperTrayEmpty)

- FALSE

State the value of (FilesWaiting > 0)

- TRUE

State the value of NOT(PaperTrayEmpty) AND (FilesWaiting > 0)

- FALSE

State the output of the algorithm

- PLEASE ADD PAPER

State the output of the algorithm when the values of the variables are as follows. Justify your answer in each case.

PaperTrayEmpty = FALSE, FilesWaiting = 1 (4)

- Output: PRINTING
- NOT(PaperTrayEmpty) is TRUE
- (FilesWaiting > 0) is TRUE
- So, overall, "IF" condition is true

PaperTrayEmpty = FALSE, FilesWaiting = 0 (4)

- Output: PLEASE ADD PAPER
- NOT(PaperTrayEmpty) is TRUE
- (FilesWaiting > 0) is FALSE
- So, overall, "IF" condition is false / "ELSE" part is executed

Rewrite the algorithm so that when PaperTrayEmpty is False and FilesWaiting is 0, the output is "STATUS OK". (The output in other cases should not change.) (4)

```
IF PaperTrayEmpty THEN
   Output 'PLEASE ADD PAPER'
ELSE
   IF FilesWaiting > 0 THEN
     Output 'PRINTING'
   ELSE
     Output 'STATUS OK'
   END IF
END IF
```

Marks for

- Tests for PaperTrayEmpty being TRUE or FALSE
- Tests for FilesWaiting being > 0 or not

And based on these tests:

- Outputs "STATUS OK" when PaperTrayEmpty = FALSE and FilesWaiting = 0
- Outputs "Please Add Paper" when PaperTrayEmpty = TRUE and FilesWaiting = 0
- Outputs "Please Add Paper" when PaperTrayEmpty = TRUE and FilesWaiting > 0
- Outputs "PRINTING ..." when PaperTrayEmpty = FALSE and FilesWaiting > 0

4.5 Understand the effects of the precedence of standard operators

Some operators are more 'important' than others. Early in your academic career you would have given the nonsense word BODMAS or something similar. BODMAS stands for Brackets Of, Division, Multiplication Addition Subtraction. BODMAS is designed to help you remember the rules of operator precedence when it comes to arithmetic. A short example should illustrate the point.

Consider the expression $x = 3 * 5 + 2$. Is the answer $17(3 * 5 = 15 + 2 = 17)$ or is the answer $21(5 + 2 = 7$ which is then multiplied by 3 to give the answer 21). Since Multiplication comes before (the technical term is 'precedes') Addition in BODMAS, it must be the case that 5 must be multiplied by 3 before 2 is added, so the answer is 17. We can alter the calculation by adding brackets as in $x = 3 * (5 + 2)$. In this case $5 + 2 = 7$ must be evaluated first before multiplying by 3 (because Brackets precede Multiplication in BODMAS).

All operators are assigned levels of precedence. At AS Level, BODMAS is sufficient with the additional proviso that arithmetic and concatenation operators all have higher precedence than comparison and logical operators. All comparison operators have equal precedence, and all have higher precedence than logical operators. Operators with equal precedence are evaluated left to right in the order in which they appear in the expression.

4.6 Evaluate expressions containing arithmetic, relational and Boolean operators and parentheses

In this section of the specification, the examiners test your understanding and ability to evaluate expressions containing a range of operators. A typical question is shown next.

A program contains the following procedure to calculate the number of tiles needed to cover a floor.

```
01 PROCEDURE solveit(L, W, T)
02 a = L DIV T
03 b = (W DIV T) + 1
04 c = a * b
05 d = c + (c DIV 10)
06 OUTPUT d
07 END PROCEDURE
```

The procedure is called as follows: solveit (400, 230, 50). State the values of the variables a, b, c, and d at the end of this procedure call. [F452 Q2 Jan 2010 (4)]

- a = 8
- b = 5

- c = 40 (examiner will allow follow through)
- d = 44 (examiner will allow follow through)

A question in a similar vein.

Consider the following algorithm

```
01 FOR  i  =  1  TO  100
02    IF  VOTE_CAST(i)  =    A    THEN
03       VOTES(1)  =  VOTES(1)  +  1
04    ELSE
05       IF  VOTE_CAST(i)  =    B    THEN
06          VOTES(2)  =  VOTES(2)  +  1
07       ELSE
08          VOTES(3)  =  VOTES(3)  +  1
09       ENDIF
10    ENDIF
11 NEXT  i
12 OUTPUT  A,B,C
```

Explain what happens when the algorithm is executed [F452 Q3 Specimen Questions (4)]

- Takes each vote in turn
- Decides whether it is A, B or C
- Keeps a running total of the number of votes for each of A, B and C
- Outputs 0,0,0 - any output given would be meaningless

Line 10 is meant to output the total votes for A, B and C. It does not work. Rewrite line 10 to produce the correct result. (2)

- OUTPUT VOTES(1), VOTES(2), VOTES(3)

4.7   Understand and use a range of operators and built-in functions for string manipulation

All languages have at least a simple range of functions that can operate on strings. We often want to *copy* strings, *compare* strings or determine the *length* of a string. If we're trying to format strings it's often useful to be able to extract the *left* part of a string, the *right* part of a string of perhaps some piece of the *middle* of the string. We might also want to work out where a particular sub phrase starts in our string. Finally, we also need to be able to convert from a character to its ASCII code and from an ASCII code to the corresponding character.

Different languages offer differing ways of manipulating strings and writing your code in Visual Basic, C, Pascal, Java or any other appropriate language is perfectly fine.

During your course you will have been taught one or more high level languages and you should have experience of using string manipulation functions in your chosen language. However, as a specific example of how you might make use of string functions, the following examples use Java as found in Processing (http://processing.org), a powerful open source Java based graphical environment.

Unlike some other languages, Java doesn't have specific functions to convert an ASCII function to its corresponding ASCII code. To perform a conversion it is sufficient to simply use an integer or char cast. For example, to find the ASCII code of the character 'A', `int codeASCII = (int)'A'` declares and initialises `codeASCII` to 65. Going the other way, to convert ASCII code 66 to its corresponding character, `char ourChar = (char)66;` declares and initialises `ourChar` to 'B'.

Most languages have functions to extract the leftmost n characters, the rightmost n characters and characters from the middle of a string. In Java this is accomplished using the `substring()` method[1] which takes two parameters, the starting character position and the length of the string we want. In addition the method `length()` when applied to a string, will as its name suggests, return the length of the string.

For example

```
String ourString = ''Charles eats a banana'';

int n = ourString.length();    // n = 21
String ourLeft = ourString.substring(0, 5); // i.e. ''Charl''
String ourRight = ourString.substring(n-5, n);  // i.e. ''anana''
String midString = ourString.substring(2, 4); // i.e. ''arle''
```

To find the character at a particular position in the string we can use the method `charAt()` on our string. `charAt()` takes one parameter, the point in the string of the character we want (remembering that we always count from zero);

For example

```
String ourString = ''Charles eats a banana'';
char ourCharacter = ourString.charAt(6); // ourCharacter = 's'
```

To find the position of a particular character within a string we can use the `indexOf()` method. This takes one parameter, the character we're trying to find.

```
String ourString = ''Charles eats a banana'';
char n = ourString.indexOf('s'); // n = 6
```

To *compare* two strings in Java, `if string1.equals(string2))` checks to see whether string1 is the same as string2.

Concatenation of strings in Java is achieved using the '+' sign. For example `String s = ''This is a '' + ''banana sandwich''` will concatenate the two strings into the single string ''This is a banana sandwich''.

It is also quite simple to split strings using Java. The solution to the following question provides an example of this. In this example, the examiners expect you to turn the flowchart into code in a language that you are familiar with. In our case, continuing with our example, this will be Java in a Processing environment.

---

[1]The term 'method' tends to be used in object orientated languages rather than the more familiar term 'function'

The software used by a telephone company includes a function which takes the duration of a call as a string and returns the length of the call in minutes. For example, if the input is 1:30 the output will be 1.5. Here is an algorithm for this function.

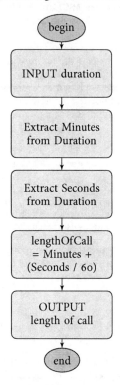

Rewrite this function in a high level language using appropriate string manipulation functions, ensuring that your code can be easily followed by another programmer. You must state the high level language that you use. [F452 Q4 Specimen Questions (6)]

```
float parseString (String incoming)
{
  String delimiter = ":";
  String[] tokens = incoming.split(delimiter);

  int minutes = Integer.parseInt (tokens[0]);
  int seconds = Integer.parseInt (tokens[1]);

  float lengthOfCall = minutes + seconds / 60.00;

  return lengthOfCall;
}


void setup()
```

```
{
  size (800,800);
  print ("Time of call is : ");
  println (parseString ("15:45"));
}
```

Let me explain how the code works.

The examiners have asked us to write a function that takes a string as an input parameter and returns a real number (these are floats in Java). I've called the function `parseString` because that's what we're doing (reading something and then chopping it up to make sense of what we've got is called parsing). It takes one parameter, a string that I've called `incoming`.

`incoming` is going to be in the form "xx:xx", and as an example we're going to parse "15:45". The ':' character is used to split the minutes and seconds - in English, this is called a 'delimiter'. Java has a method called `split` that operates on strings and will split them up into their components according to the delimiter that you give it.

Our delimiter is the character ':', so we write the statement `String delimiter = ''':''`. When the string is split up we'll end up with at least (and in our case, exactly) two strings so we need to reserve some string storage for them. This is why the next line declares an array of Strings called `tokens`. The line `String[] tokens = incoming.split(delimiter);` splits up the string `incoming` according to where the delimiter (in this case ':') is.

After this method call we'll end up with two strings, the first, the minutes stored in `tokens[0]` and the second, the seconds stored in `tokens[1]`. Note that these are strings, so we need to convert them to integers before we can do any calculations with them. This is the purpose of the next two lines, `int minutes = Integer.parseInt (tokens[0]);` and `int seconds = Integer.parseInt (tokens[1]);`. The method `parseInt` operating on the class integer takes one parameter, a string which it converts to an integer. After these two lines we now know the minutes and seconds and so we can work out the length of the call by a simple calculation, done by `float lengthOfCall = minutes + seconds / 60.00;`.

We finish off by simply returning the value we've calculated where it is immediately printed using the Processing function `println`.

The examiners were looking for the following.

- Function takes a string as input
- The number of minutes is correctly extracted from the input string (i.e. all the characters before the colon)
- The number of seconds is correctly extracted from the input string (i.e. all the characters after the colon/last two characters)
- The extracted strings are correctly converted into integers (or other numeric type)
- The length of call is correctly calculated
- The length of call is returned (as a real number)
- Appropriate identifier names used throughout
- Code is annotated and can be easily followed

Bus tickets have three lines of 15 characters. Each line is formatted into a single string and then printed. An example ticket is shown below.

R	O	U	T	E		N	9	3			·			
A	V	E	N	U	E		-	K	I	N	G	S	W	A
A	D	U	L	T						£	0	.	4	0

The first line contains the word ROUTE followed by a space followed by the value of RouteNumber. Using string manipulation operations in a high level language you have studied, show how the line can be formatted into a single string. [F452 Q1 Jan 2011 (2)]

- Concatenation/recognisable concatenation operator used …
- …on ROUTE and RouteNumber
- Java example : RouteCode = "ROUTE " + RouteNumber; (if RouteCode is a `String`)

In the second line the names of the stops are printed using 7 characters each. If a name is shorter than 7 characters, spaces are added. If a name is longer than 7 characters, any extra characters are removed. Show how string manipulation functions can be used to format the name of a stop for printing. You do not need to format the whole line. (3)

- find the length of the name of the stop
- If length ≥ 7, extract the first 7 characters (e.g. Use the LEFT() function)
- If length is < 7 append spaces to bring length up to 7

In the third line the ticket type is printed on the left and the fare (preceded by £) is printed on the right. Explain how string manipulation functions can be used to format the values of TicketType and Fare into a correct 15-character string for printing. (5)

- Determine length of Ticket Type
- Format Fare to Currency/to 2 d.p.with £ sign
- Determine length of formatted fare
- Calculate number of spaces needed (15 - length of other strings)
- Concatenate TicketType, spaces and (formatted) fare

A parcel delivery company has a website where customers can arrange for parcels to be collected and delivered. Drivers in the company need the postcodes sorted in ascending order. A computer program sorts the postcodes, as strings, in ascending order. The table below shows a sample of the data entered by customers, the result after the program sorts the data and what the drivers need.

Postcodes entered by customers	Postcodes after the program sorts them	Postcodes in the order that the drivers need them
BF1 3UY	BF1 3UY	BF1 2AJ
BF21 1XX	BF12AJ	BF1 3UY
BF12AJ	BF18 4TZ	BF2 0ED
BF2 0GH	BF2 0GH	BF2 0GH
BF18 4TZ	BF21 1XX	BF18 4TZ
bf2 oed	bf2 oed	BF21 1XX

A different solution to the problem is to write a program to reformat the postcode entered by the customer before it is sorted. Describe the operations that the program will have to do in order to convert the postcodes to a format which will be sorted correctly. You should refer to string manipulation functions and operations in a high level language you have studied. The quality of written communication will be assessed in your answer to this

question. [F452 Q2 Jun 2009 (6)]

To get full marks for this question, the examiners expect that candidates will show a clear understanding of the question and give a detailed description of the reformatting to be done and how this can be achieved. They also expect that the information will be presented in a structured and coherent form, there will be few if any errors in spelling, grammar and punctuation and technical terms will be used appropriately and correctly. They would expect at a minimum for the following four points to be included.

- Convert all lowercase characters to uppercase
- A space character needs to be inserted if there isn't one before the last three characters
- A space character/0 could also be inserted before the first digit IF there is only one digit in the first half of the post code
- All of these with correct indication of functions/operations which will be needed.

4.8   UNDERSTAND THAT RELATIONAL OPERATIONS ON ALPHANUMERIC STRINGS DEPEND ON CHARACTER CODES OF THE CHARACTERS

This section of the specification will test that you understand that each character has a unique ASCII code. The examiners also assume that you have at least a rough idea of the standard ASCII table. In particular they will expect you to know that the numbers have lower ASCII codes than uppercase characters which in turn have lower ASCII codes than lowercase characters. This leads to situations where for example, 'XYZ' < 'abc', '2' > '17' and '3' <> '3.0'. They might even assume as in one of the questions in this section that you know that the ASCII code for 'A' is 65 and they might assume that you know that each lower case character has an ASCII code 32 higher than that of its corresponding uppercase characters. So for example whereas the ASCII code for 'A' is 65, the ASCII code for 'a' will be 65 + 32 = 97.

In the table in the previous section, repeated below, explain, using examples, why the order of the postcodes sorted by the program is different from the order wanted by the drivers.
[F452 Q2 Jun 2009 (6)]

Postcodes entered by customers	Postcodes after the program sorts them	Postcodes in the order that the drivers need them
BF1 3UY	BF1 3UY	BF1 2AJ
BF21 1XX	BF12AJ	BF1 3UY
BF12AJ	BF18 4TZ	BF2 0ED
BF2 0GH	BF2 0GH	BF2 0GH
BF18 4TZ	BF21 1XX	BF18 4TZ
bf2 oed	bf2 oed	BF21 1XX

- Characters are compared from left to right
- ...using their character (ASCII) codes
- The character with the lower code comes first
- Subsequent character used only if the two characters compared are equal
- Upper case characters come before lower case characters in the ASCII table
- ...e.g. 0G comes before 0e
- The space character has a lower character code than all letters

- ...so the presence of a space changes the position of the post code
- Any numbers are sorted by digit from left to right instead of the number's value
- ...e.g. BF1, BF12, BF18, BF2

Numerology is a method of fortune-telling where letters are converted into numbers. A programmer is writing an application to carry out this conversion. The application contains the function PositionInAlphabet() which takes a single upper case letter as an argument and returns the position of that letter in the alphabet. For example PositionInAlphabet(. **= 1 and** PositionInAlphabet(J) = 10. **Here is the code for this function.**

```
01 FUNCTION PositionInAlphabet(Letter : CHARACTER) : INTEGER
02   CharCode = ASCII(Letter)
03   PositionInAlphabet = CharCode - 64
04 END FUNCTION
```

In line 02, a built-in string manipulation function, ASCII, has been used. Describe what the function ASCII does. [F452 Q4 Jun 2010 (2)]

- Takes a single character
- ...and returns its ASCII code/character code in the computers character set

Explain why it is necessary to subtract 64 in line 03. (2)

- The ASCII/Character codes for letters A-Z do not start from 1...
- ...but start (in this case) from 65 / 65 is the ASCII code for A ...
- ...and continue in sequence to Z
- Subtracting 64 corrects this offset.

4.9 INPUT AND VALIDATE DATA

Validation means checking that data is reasonable and complete. Validation checks include the following.

- *Presence check.* Is the data present, has the field required been filled?
- *Length check.* Is the data of a reasonable length, for example is a user name between 5 and 15 characters long?
- *Format check.* Is the data of the correct format? E.g. a date might need to be in the form dd/mm/yyyy
- *Range check.* Is data in the correct range? E.g. a pensioner is someone over the age of 65 and (presumably) younger than say 120.
- *Existence check.* Does the data that has been entered match a previously recorded value. E.g. does entering flight code AZ854 match a flight that actually exists.

Explain the term validation. [F452 Q2 Jun 2009 (2)]

- Input data is checked by the computer
- ...against a set of rules
- ...to ensure that it is reasonable/sensible

Drivers in a company use postcodes sorted in ascending order. A computer program sorts the postcodes, as strings, in ascending order. Describe three validation checks that can be used on the postcode. (6)

- Presence check
- …that a postcode has been entered.
- Length check
- …the postcode should be 7 or 8 characters long (including space).
- Character check
- …check that it is an uppercase characters
- …or digit/space.

Writing maintainable programs

5.1 DEFINE, UNDERSTAND AND USE THE TERMS VARIABLE, CONSTANT, IDENTIFIER, RESERVED WORD/KEYWORD

A *variable* 'is the identifier or name associated with a particular memory location which is used to store data'[1]. *Local variables* are defined only within the scope of the section of code in which they are declared. They are destroyed and their contents lost when control moves outside their scope. *Global variables* can be used anywhere within the program. Their contents are accessible throughout the code. Although this is very occasionally a good thing, good programming practice will avoid the use of global variables as far as possible.

A *constant* is a data item with a fixed value. It does not change as the program is executed.

An *identifier* 'is a name or label chosen by the programmer to represent an object within a program. The object could be a variable, a function, a procedure or any element defined within a program'.[2]

A *reserved word* or *keyword* is 'any word in the vocabulary of a programming language which can only have the meaning which is defined in the language'.[3]

A programmer is producing a computer program which allocates seats to customers in a small theatre. The code for the program uses variables and constants. Describe what is meant by a variable. [F452 Q4 Jun 2009 (2)]

- An identifier/name ... associated with a particular memory location
- It is used to store (and manipulate) data ... which can be changed while the program is running

State how a constant is different from a variable. (1)

- When a constant is declared it must be given a value.
- The value cannot be changed while the program is running.

---

[1] BCS - A glossary of computing terms
[2] Ibid.
[3] Ibid.

A mail order company charges for delivery depending on the volume and the weight of the items purchased. A computer program processes orders and calculates the cost of delivery. Here is an extract from the program.

```
01  BEGIN PROGRAM
02
03    VARIABLE TotalWeight : REAL
04    VARIABLE TotalVolume : REAL
05
06    PROCEDURE CalculateTotals()
07
08      VARIABLE i : INTEGER
09
10      TotalWeight = 0
11      TotalVolume = 0
```

In line 03 of this extract, TotalWeight is declared as a global variable. Describe what is meant by a variable. [F452 Q4 Jan 2010 (3)]

- An identifier/ name
- …used to refer to a particular memory location
- …used to store data (which is used by the program)
- The data stored may change while the program is running
- Allows the algorithm to be written even when the data is not yet known

5.2   EXPLAIN THE NEED FOR GOOD PROGRAM-WRITING TECHNIQUES TO FACILITATE ONGOING MAINTENANCE OF PROGRAMS

Describe two program writing techniques that can be used in the code of a program to facilitate ongoing maintenance. [F452 Q4 Specimen Questions (4)]

- Use of meaningful variable names
- …to allow others to understand scope of variables
- …also applies to names of functions/procedures.
- Indentation of code/spacing of code
- …to show clearly the lines of code which should be treated together
- …typically loops/selection.
- Annotate code
- …with comments that are not used by the computer
- …so that others can understand reasons for code/structures

Explain why a programmer should use good programming techniques when writing code. [F452 Q4 Jan 2009 (6)]

- Enables teams of programmers to work collaboratively
- …code split into modules / blocks which are easier to maintain / debug individually
- …conventions used to ensure everyone understands program
- Code can easily be read by other programmers / at a future date
- …Indentation clearly shows structure of code
- …meaningful identifiers make code easier to read / understand
- Program is less error prone
- …it is internally documented / comments can be compared with logic

- ...and is easier to trace / debug
- ..... code is easier to read/closer to pseudocode

5.3 DECLARE VARIABLES AND CONSTANTS, UNDERSTANDING THE EFFECT OF SCOPE

Declaring variables and constants simply tell the compiler to reserve space for them. So for example, when you write int n you are telling the compiler that you want space reserved for an integer (usually 4 characters) that you are going to refer to in the future as 'n'. When you give n a value, you *initialise* it. This can often be done in a single step.

For example int n = 75, declares and initialises n in a single line.

Local variables only hold scope in the block of code in which they are declared. *Global* variables are declared at the start of a program and hold scope throughout the whole of the program.

It is important to be careful when you choose variable names. Names such as string or for or while clearly cannot be used as variable names since they are *reserved* for use by the programming language itself. These are examples of *reserved words* or *keywords*. See page 73 for definitions.

A mail order company charges for delivery depending on the volume and the weight of the items purchased. A computer program processes orders and calculates the cost of delivery. Here is an extract from the program.

```
01 BEGIN PROGRAM
02
03    VARIABLE TotalWeight : REAL
04    VARIABLE TotalVolume : REAL
05
06    PROCEDURE CalculateTotals()
07
08       VARIABLE i : INTEGER
09
```

Identify one global variable and one local variable declared in the extract shown. [F452 Q4 Jan 2010 (2)]

- Global variable: TotalVolume
- Local variable: i

Explain the difference between a global variable and a local variable. (4)

- A global variable is declared at the beginning of a program
- ...and is available throughout the program
- A local variable is declared within a subprogram/ procedure/function/block of code
- ...and is only available within that section of code
- ...and is destroyed/deleted when the subprogram exits A local variable can override a global variable (with the same name)

Explain and justify the best practice when declaring variables and constants in code, to ensure error-free and easily understandable code. [F452 Q3 Jun 2010 (8)]

- Identifier names should describe the item identified
- …for example RowNumber, ColumnNumber
- …so that the code can be read and understood without referring to a lookup table
- Declarations should be made obvious within the code
- …for example by using comments with explanations of their purpose
- …or separating them from code with blank lines
- …so that they can easily be found, if you need to refer to them while reading the code
- Standard conventions should be used
- …such as CamelCase/underscores/type prefixes
- …as most translators do not allow spaces in identifier names/as a reminder of the data type of the variable or constant
- Keyword/reserved words in the language should be avoided
- …e.g. you should not have a variable called Print/Count/Array/ other suitable example …
- …the translator will interpret this as the keyword and produce a syntax error
- Declare constants and use these in the code instead of literals
- …e.g. use NumberOfRows = 3, NumberOfColumns = 9 in this case
- …code is easier to understand because the name of the constant rather than a literal is used (e.g for i = 1 to NumberOfRows)
- …if the value changes, you only need to change it in the declaration of the constant (eg to print tickets with 4 or 5 rows) instead of looking for every instance of the literal
- Variables/Constants should be declared as local wherever possible
- …reducing the scope/lifetime of the variable to the minimum necessary
- …avoiding errors due to clashing variable names in different parts of the program
- Initialise variables when declared (in languages which allow this)
- …e.g. int i = 1; string New = "";
- …this ensures that a suitable value is in the variable at the start of your algorithm

5.4   SELECT AND USE MEANINGFUL IDENTIFIER NAMES AND USE STANDARD CONVENTIONS TO SHOW THE DATA TYPES AND ENHANCE READABILITY

A program contains the following procedure to calculate the number of tiles needed to cover a floor. This procedure has parameters.

```
01 PROCEDURE solveit(L, W, T)
02 a = L DIV T
03 b = (W DIV T) + 1
04 c = a * b
05 d = c + (c DIV 10)
06 OUTPUT d
07 END PROCEDURE
```

Explain and justify how the code for this procedure can be rewritten to make it easier to maintain. [F452 Q2 Jan 2010 (8)]

The examiners would expect to see the following points to be made.

- Variables and procedures should be given more descriptive names such as length, width, tile/findNumberOfTiles, etc using consistent conventions making it easier to tell what the variables represent/procedures do

- Code should be indented to show program constructs/blocks for example PROCE-DURE/END PROCEDURE making it easier to trace the code and check for incorrect blocks
- Comments should be added to the code and the code separated into logical sections making it easier to read

For example

```
//
// Calculates number of tiles needed for floor
// Parameters :
// IN : floorLength, floorWidth, tileSize
// OUT : number of tilesNeeded
//
PROCEDURE numberOfTiles (floorLength, floorWidth, tileSize)
// calculate number of tiles needed for the length
  tilesNeededForLength = floorLength DIV tileSize

// calculate number of tiles needed for the width
  tilesNeededForWidth = (floorWidth DIV tileSize) + 1

// multiply to get number of tiles required
  tilesNeeded = tilesNeededForLength * tilesNeededForWidth

// Make sure we have some spare by adding 10%
  tilesNeeded = tilesNeeded + (tilesNeeded DIV 10)

// return the number of tiles required
  OUTPUT tilesNeeded
07 END PROCEDURE
```

The design for a computer program contains the following algorithm shown in pseudo-code.

```
01 INPUT A
02 INPUT B
03 C = 0
04 IF A = B THEN
05    B = 1
06 ELSE
07    WHILE B > A
08      B= B  A
09      C=C+ 1
10    END WHILE
11    A = B
12 END IF
```

Good program writing techniques make pseudo-code easier to follow. Explain one technique used in the pseudo-code to make it easier to follow. [F452 Q3 Jan 2011 (2)]

- Indentation of
- …blocks of code which are included within a control structure
- …allows you to see clearly where the structure starts and ends
- Suitable example from code

5.5   Use declared constants to improve maintainability

Describe how using constants can help improve the maintainability of the code. [F452 Q4 Jun 2009 (2)]

- A descriptive identifier/name is used for the constant
- ...which makes the code clearer to read and understand (during maintenance)
- ...and it is easier to remember the identifier than the value when writing code
- If the value needs to be changed then only one change needs to be made (where the constant is declared)
- This updates the value throughout the program

To calculate the fare in a program calculating the cost of a bus journey, the program uses the following function.

```
01 FUNCTION CalculateFare(Start, Destination, Type)
02    CONSTANT PensionerMax = 0.50
03    Distance = Destination    Start
04    Fare = Distance * 0.20
05    IF Type = 'CHILD' THEN
06       Fare = Fare / 2
07    END IF
08    IF Type = 'PENSIONER' AND Fare > PensionerMax
09       Fare = PensionerMax
10    END IF
11    RETURN Fare
12 END FUNCTION
```

The function declares and uses the constant PensionerMax. State two advantages of declaring and using this constant. [F452 Q1 Jan 2011 (2)]

- If the value of PensionerMax changes, this only needs to be updated once (on line 2)
- ...and the new value will be used throughout the code
- The statements (on lines 8 and 9) are clearer because we know what the value represents
- Cannot be accidentally changed/will be consistent throughout the program.

Identify one other value in the code for which a constant could be used, and state a suitable name for this constant. (2)

- 0.20 (on line 4) ...suitable identifier e.g. CostPerStop
- 2 (on line 6) ...suitable identifier e.g. DivisorForChildFare

5.6   Initialise variables appropriately, before using them

It is good programming practice to initialise variables before using them. This guarantees that a variable will hold a known value before first use.

The following algorithm finds the total of all the digits in a number.

```
01 INPUT
02 T = 0
03 WHILE N>0
04 L = N MOD 10
```

```
05 R = N DIV 10
06 T = T + L
07 N = R
08 END WHILE
```

Explain the purpose of the instruction in line 02. [F452 Q4 Jan 2009 (2)]

- Initialise T (to its starting value/0)
- Before it is used in an expression (in line 6)
- Or else it might use a value retained from previous uses of T

The design for a computer program contains the following algorithm shown in pseudo-code.

```
01 INPUT A
02 INPUT B
03 C = 0
04 IF A = B THEN
05    B = 1
06 ELSE
07    WHILE B > A
08       B = B  A
09       C = C+ 1
10    END WHILE
11    A = B
12 END IF
```

Explain why line 03 is needed in this algorithm.

- Initialise the value of C
- ...before it is used (in line 09)
- ...otherwise previous values of C will lead to wrong results

An array VOTES contains three integers. In pseudo-code or a language of your choice, write a FOR loop to initialise the array. [F452 Q3 Specimen Questions (4)]

- Use of FOR loop
- ...with correct condition
- Attempt to set values to 0
- ...using correct subscript

e.g.

```
FOR J = 1 to 3
  VOTES(J) = 0
NEXT J
```

5.7 Use annotation, indentation and formatting

Annotation (or commenting) a program is an essential element of good programming practice. It is not necessary to annotate every line of a program especially if the programmer has chosen sensible variable and function names but every algorithm, every subroutine and every important section of code should be extensively annotated. Good annotation means that the

any programmer (including the original author) can pick up the code and quickly work out the purpose of each piece of code.

Indentation is another essential element - code that uses selection extensively is pretty much unreadable without indentation.

Using *meaningful variable names* is an important aspect of good programming practice. Professional programmers spend a great deal of their time choosing their identifiers. Well chosen identifiers for variables and functions help enormously in understanding what the code does and as mentioned above, good identifiers cut down on the amount of annotation required.

The design for a computer program contains the following algorithm shown in pseudo-code.

```
01  INPUT  A
02  INPUT  B
03  C  =  0
04  IF  A  =  B  THEN
05     B  =  1
06  ELSE
07     WHILE  B  >  A
08        B  =  B  -  A
09        C  =  C  +  1
10     END  WHILE
11     A  =  B
12  END  IF
```

Explain one technique not used in the pseudo-code which could make it easier to follow.
[F452 Q3 Jan 2011 (2)] *Either*

- Use of meaningful identifiers
- ...instead of A, B, C
- ...which tell us what the values represent

Or

- Use of comments
- ...which explain the steps of the algorithm to the reader
- ...but are not to be executed

The following algorithm finds the total of all the digits in a number.

```
01  INPUT
02  T  =  0
03  WHILE  N>0
04  L  =  N  MOD  10
05  R  =  N  DIV  10
06  T  =  T  +  L
07  N  =  R
08  END  WHILE
```

One way to improve the readability of the algorithm is to include comments. Describe two other ways to improve the readability of the algorithm. [F452 Q4 Jan 2009 (4)]

- Use indentation
- ...on lines 04,05,06,07 to identify the WHILE loop clearly
- Use meaningful identifiers/names for the variables
- ...so you do not need to remember what they are / make code easier

Testing and running a solution

6.1 Describe types of errors in programs

Programmers make errors. Some errors are caught by the compiler. More serious errors cause the program to crash whilst others, often more difficult to find are noticed because the code does something unexpected. Errors can be classified as follows.

Run-time errors are errors detected when the program runs and often causes the program to halt or crash. These are typically caused by arithmetic errors where a number overflows or an attempt is made to divide by zero.

Syntax errors occur when the program does not follow the rules of the programming language. Incorrectly nested control structures, incorrectly spelled reserved words are examples of this type of error. Syntax errors are picked up by the compiler.

Logic errors occur when the design of an algorithm is flawed, such as an inappropriate comparison statement. For example, if the programmer wrote if (A>B) when if (A>=B) should have been written.

Name and describe one type of error which can occur in a program, stating when it would be detected. [F452 Q3 Jan 2010 (3)]

- Syntax (error)
- When the program is translated

Or

- Logic Error
- …does not perform the algorithm intended by the programmer/suitable example
- …detected when program produces incorrect result

Or

- Run-time error
- …statement in the code cannot be executed (due to effects not catered for by the program)/division by zero /overflow/lack of memory/unusual data
- …detected when the program crashes

A company is producing a computer program for a new cash point. Here is part of the code for the program. This code contains some errors.

```
01 PROCEDURE WithdrawCash(AccountNo:INTEGER)
02    VARIABLE Amount:REAL //how much to withdraw
03    VARIABLE Print:BOOLEAN //whether a receipt is wanted
04    Amount = GetAmountWanted()
05    Print = GetWhetherReceiptWanted()
06    IF Balance(AccountNo) < Amount THEN
07       DispenseCash(Amount)
08       IF Print = TRUE THEN
09          PrintReceipt(AccountNo, Amount)
10       END IF
11    ELSE
12       OUTPUT 'Insufficient Funds'
13    END IF
14 END PROCEDURE
```

When the code is tested, the variable Print causes a keyword violation error. Describe what is meant by a keyword. [F452 Q2 Jun 2011 (2)]

- Words which are already used for a purpose within the language
- A reserved word/ cannot be used as an identifier (for a variable, subroutine etc ...)

State why this keyword violation is a syntax error. (1)

- It breaks the rules of the language

There is also an error in line 06. State the error and what the implication is to the customer. (2)

- Cash is dispensed only if the customer does not have enough money/when the balance is less than the amount wanted
- Customers will go overdrawn/will not be able to withdraw money they have in the bank

State what type of error this is. (1)

- Logic error

A computer program contains the following instructions.

```
01 INPUT X
02 INPUT Y
03 Z = -1
04 REPEAT
05    Z=Z+1
06    Y=Y-X
07 UNTIL Y < 0
08 OUTPUT Z
```

The program is given the inputs: -4, 12. Explain why this will produce an error and state the type of error it will produce. [F452 Q1 Jun 2009 (3)]

- There is an infinite loop
- ...because repeated subtraction of -4 from Y makes it bigger / Y will never be < 0
- Eventually Y will be too large to be stored

- ...causing the program to crash
- Run-time error

A utilities company provides both gas and electricity. Customers whose bills when added together exceed 10 are given a 5% discount on this total. The following code has been written to calculate the total bill of customers including the discount, if any.

```
01 INPUT GasBill
02 INPUT ElectricBill
03 If GasBill AND ElectricBill > 10 THEN
04    TotalBill = GasBill + ElectricBill * 0.95
05 Else
06    TotalBill = GasBill + ElectricBill
07 END IF
```

This code contains an error in line 03 and another error in line 04. Explain why there is an error in line 03 and state the type of error. (3)

- AND operator has higher precedence than >
- ...so it will do (GasBill AND ElectricBill) > 10
- ...but GasBill and ElectricBill are not boolean expressions/they are numbers
- ...which should have been added
- Syntax error (referring to ANDing numerals) / logic error (referring to AND instead of +)

Explain why there is an error in line 04 and state the type of error. (3)

- * operator has higher precedence than +
- So it will do (ElectricBill * 0.95) + GasBill / the discount will only be applied to the Electricity bill
- ...instead of (Electric Bill + GasBill) * 0.95
- Logic error.

6.2   Describe testing strategies

There are various testing strategies. The questions that follow cover them pretty clearly.

Before releasing software, it is tested using a variety of strategies. Describe (a) Black box testing, (b) White box testing (c) Alpha testing, (c) Beta testing and (d) Acceptance testing. [F452 Q2 Jan 2009 (2,2,2,2,2)]

Black box testing

- (Suitable) inputs are tested
- ...against the expected output (according to the design)
- ...without considering how the program works

White box testing

- The actual steps of the algorithm are tested
- ...to make sure all parts work as intended
- All possible paths through the algorithm need to be tested

Alpha testing

- Testing is carried out by the programmer(s)/ software company
- ...playing the role of the user
- ...during development
- ...to find bugs in the program

Beta testing

- The nearly complete program
- ...is given to a group of users to test/is tested under normal operating conditions/tested by people who were not involved in the production
- The aim is to find any bugs which the programmer has overlooked

Acceptance testing

- The program is tested to prove to the end user
- ...that the program works correctly
- Meets the original objectives
- After development is complete
- Before handing it over / end user will pay if satisfied

Explain the difference between beta-testing and acceptance testing. [F452 Q4 Jan 2010 (4)]

In beta-testing

- The nearly complete program
- ...is given to a group of users to test/is tested under normal operating conditions/tested by people who were not involved in the production
- The aim is to find any bugs which the programmer has overlooked

In acceptance testing

- The program is considered complete
- The programmer demonstrates the working program to the client
- The aim is to show that the program meets all the requirements of the client.

Explain the difference between white box testing and a black box testing. [F452 Q3 Jan 2011 (4)]

In white box testing

- The actual steps of the algorithm are tested
- ...to make sure all parts work as intended
- All possible paths through the algorithm must be tested

In black box testing

- Sets of inputs are tested
- ...to see if they produce the intended outputs
- You need to test all possible types of input/situations
- ...but how the algorithm works is not considered

Wayne is writing an application for a touch screen mobile phone to identify types of lady-bird. Wayne decides to release a beta version of the application. Explain the use of beta versions, and the advantages and disadvantages of their use in this case. The quality of written communication will be assessed in your answer to this question. [F452 Q1 Jun 2011 (8)]

How it is used

- Beta version is test version of the application
- … nearly complete and already tested by Wayne
- Wayne makes the application available to small group of testers
- Testers use the program as normal/in the field to identify ladybirds
- They report any errors in the program, such as functions which do not work, ladybirds found outside the expected range, incompatibility issues with other software on their phones
- May also report on desirable improvements
- Wayne tries to replicate and then solve these errors and may release updates/fixes/-workarounds to the beta testers

Advantages & disadvantages

- Application is tested using real data, some of which may not have been anticipated by Wayne when he was testing it
- Application will be tested in a number of different phones possibly with different configurations
- Consequently the final version will be more robust
- However, beta application may cause damage to testers equipment due to unexpected feature
- Wayne should ask the beta testers to agree to test the software at their own risk

6.3 SELECT SUITABLE TEST DATA FOR A GIVEN PROBLEM, INCLUDING NORMAL, BORDERLINE AND INVALID DATA

In order to fully test a program it is essential that not only is the program tested on data that the program expects to receive, but it is also tested on data that it is not expected to receive. To do this the program should first be tested with normal data to make sure that it performs correctly on data that it can expect to get when running normally.

It should also be given borderline data that is just within the normal range. Programmers often make slight but important errors which show up when tested with borderline data. For example, the programmer might be testing whether $A > B$ when he or she should have been testing whether $A >= B$. Borderline data will identify this type of error.

Additionally the program should be tested with invalid data, for example by entered data outside the expected range, perhaps by inputting a string of characters instead of the expected real number. Well written programs will detect such inputs and deal with them gracefully, usually by politely reminding the user that a real number is expected.

Note that it is notoriously difficult to test one's own program. Having taken such trouble over writing it, the programmer is extremely loath to break it and simply will not test the program properly. Not so friends and colleagues who will do everything they can to break it. This is why in most professional software companies there is a small group whose sole role is to test their colleague's programs to destruction.

A program is written which will use as input the marks gained by candidates in an AS examination paper. The top mark possible is 100. The program will calculate the mean (average) mark and output the highest mark, the lowest mark and the mean. It is decided to test the module using groups of four test marks at a time. Explain why the testing was carried out using only four marks at a time. [F452 Q2 Specimen Questions (2)]

- Manageable number for input
- Expected results can be calculated easily

Using the table below, give three separate test cases for testing the program. (9)

Input Data	Reason for test	Expected Result

Answer :

Input Data	Reason for test	Expected Result
10, 20, 30, 40	Normal data	40, 10, 25
0, 20, 30, 100	Borderline values	100, 0, 37.5
0, 20, 30, 101	Invalid values	Error message

A program calculates the cost of parking at the city councils car parks as follows.
- **Free from 5am to 8am**
- **3 per hour or part of an hour between 8am and 5pm**
- **Free from 5pm to 12 midnight**
- **No parking from 12 midnight to 5am**

Fill in the table below with test data for three different tests that can be used to test whether the program charges the correct amount when given valid start and finish times. For each set of data, state the purpose of that test and the expected outcome. [F452 Q2 Jan 2009 (9)]

Start	Finish	Reason for Test	Expected

The examiners expected that the test data would include three of the following.

- Start and finish before 8 am
- Start and finish after 5 pm
- Start before 8 am and finish between 8 am and 5 pm
- Start and finish between 8 am and 5 pm
- Start between 8 am and 5 pm and finish after 5 pm
- Start before 8 am and finish after 5 pm
- Test involving 8 am boundary
- Test involving 5am boundary

- Test fractions of an hour
- Start or finish time between 12 midnight and 5 am

Our table might look something like this.

Start	Finish	Reason for Test	Expected
08:30	15:30	Normal paid time	£21
07:00	12:00	Free and Paid	£12
05:00	24:00	Check boundaries	£27

A computer program is designed to store the results of matches in a football competition and calculate the ranking of the teams. When the results are entered, the number of points of each team are updated as follows:

- **If both teams have the same number of goals (draw) then each team gets 1 point.**
- **If one team has more goals than the other (i.e. there is a winner) then the winning team gets 3 points, and the losing team gets 0 points.**

The program is to be tested using black box testing. One possible test case is shown in the table below. Complete the table opposite with FOUR different test cases. You may use Team A and Team B as team names in your test cases. [F452 Q1 Jun 2010 (12)]

Reason for test	Test data	Expected outcome
Normal score where the first team is the winning team	Team A 2 Team B 0	Team A has 3 more points Team B's points unchanged

The examiners expected that the test data would include four of the following.

- second team has more goals than first team
- both teams have the same number of goals
- the input for number of goals of one of the teams is missing
- the input for number of goals of one of the teams is negative
- the input for number of goals of one of the teams contains a decimal fraction
- the input for number of goals of one of the teams is non-numeric
- the input for number of goals of one of the teams is a large integer
- the same team has been entered twice
- the input for number of goals is extreme/unusually high

6.4 PERFORM A DRY RUN ON A GIVEN ALGORITHM, USING A TRACE TABLE

A simple and effective method of testing an algorithm is to perform one or more *dry runs* through the data using a *trace table*. A dry run is simply short hand for 'running through the program manually with pen and paper'. The trace table is simply a table which records the values of each of the variables as they change throughout the course of the algorithm. The following questions should make this clear.

A mail order company charges for delivery depending on the volume and the weight of the items purchased. A computer program processes orders and calculates the cost of delivery. The code for calculating the total weight and the total volume of the items purchased is shown below.

```
10 TotalWeight = 0
11 TotalVolume = 0
12
13 FOR i = 1 TO NumberOfItemsOrdered
14    TotalWeight = TotalWeight + WeightOfItem(i)
15    TotalVolume = TotalVolume + VolumeOfItem(i)
16 NEXT i
```

A dry run uses the following test data:

NumberOfItemsOrdered = 2
WeightOfItem(1) = 0.3
VolumeOfItem(1) = 200
WeightOfItem(2) = 0.1
VolumeOfItem(2) = 150

Complete the trace table below, showing each line of the algorithm which will be executed. On each line, write down the new values of any variables that are changed. [F452 Q4 Jan 2010 (9)]

Line of Code Executed	Variables Changed		
	i	TotalWeight	TotalVolume

Answer :

Line of Code Executed	Variables Changed		
	i	TotalWeight	TotalVolume
10		0	
11			0
13	1		
14		0.3	
15			200
16	2		
13			
14		0.4	
15			350
16	3		
13			

A computer program contains the following instructions.

```
INPUT X
INPUT Y
Z = -1
```

```
REPEAT
   Z = Z + 1
   Y = Y - X
UNTIL Y < 0
OUTPUT Z
```

For each of the following sets of input data, complete the table below showing the values of the variables X, Y and Z after the instructions have been executed, and the output. [F452 Q1 Jun 2009 (12)]

INPUTS	X	Y	X	OUTPUT
3, 9				
5, 7				
8, 2				

Answer

INPUTS	X	Y	X	OUTPUT
3, 9	3	-3	3	3
5, 7	5	-3	1	1
8, 2	8	-6	0	0

Explain what this algorithm does. (2)

- Division of Y by X
- Integer division/rounded down
- ... using repeated subtraction

The design for a computer program contains the following algorithm shown in pseudo-code.

```
01 INPUT A
02 INPUT B
03 C = 0
04 IF A = B THEN
05    B = 1
06 ELSE
07    WHILE B > A
08       B = B - A
09       C = C + 1
10    END WHILE
11    A = B
12 END IF
```

The algorithm is tested with the inputs 2, 5. The path of execution is:
01, 02, 03, 04(FALSE), 06, 07(TRUE), 08, 09, 10, 07(TRUE), 08, 09, 10, 07(FALSE), 11, 12.

The final values of the variables A, B and C are: A =1, B = 1, C = 2

For the following sets of inputs state the path of execution. If line 04 or line 07 is executed, you should state whether the condition is TRUE or FALSE. Also state the final values of A, B and C.

Inputs : 10, 10 [F452 Q3 Jan 2011 (4)]

PATH

- 01, 02, 03, 04(TRUE)
- 05
- (06) , 12

VALUES

- A = 10, B = 1, C =0

Inputs : 4, 6 (5)

PATH

- 01, 02, 03, 04(FALSE)
- 06, 07(TRUE)
- 08, 09, 10,
- 07(FALSE), 11, 12/ 07(FALSE), 10, 11, 12

VALUES

- A = 2, B = 2, C = 1

Describe the set of input data which will produce the following path of execution using an example.

01, 02, 03, 04(FALSE), 06, 07(FALSE), 11, 12 (2)

- The first input (A) is greater than the second input (B)
- Any suitable example

A sequence of numbers begins 2, 4, 7, ... Here is an algorithm in pseudo-code for a function which returns the nth number of the sequence. For example, SequenceItem(3) returns the 3rd number in the sequence.

```
01 FUNCTION SequenceItem(n:INTEGER) : INTEGER
02    Answer = 1
03    FOR i = 1 TO n
04       Answer = Answer + i
05    NEXT i
06    RETURN Answer
07 END FUNCTION
```

Using the algorithm complete the trace table to calculate the value of SequenceItem(5).
[F452 Q4 Jun 2011 (6)]

n	i	Answer

Answer :

n	i	Answer
5		1
	1	2
	2	4
	3	7
	4	11
	5	16

6.5 DESCRIBE THE USE OF A RANGE OF DEBUGGING TOOLS

Describe debugging tools and facilities available in programming languages, which can be used to identify and correct errors in computer programs. [F452 Q1 Jun 2009 (6)]

- Translator diagnostics pick up (especially) syntax errors and informs the programmer who can then correct the error and translate again (but sometimes the error messages are incorrect/in the wrong place)
- Break points cause the program to halt in execution at strategic points current values of variables can then be checked
- Watches cause the program to halt in execution if a condition is met such as a variable changing
- Stepping — executing the code one statement at a time observing path of execution and changes to variables. Can be used with break points or watches

6.6 DESCRIBE THE PURPOSE OF AN INSTALLATION ROUTINE

The purpose of an installation routine is to ensure that all elements of a particular application are correctly installed on a customer's computer system. Modern programs typically include many files in addition to the application itself. These might include graphic files, help files, font resources, videos, dynamic link libraries and audio files. All of these need to be placed in appropriate directories on the target system so that they can be called upon by the application when required. Installation routines can be quite complex programs in their own right.

When a program is completed, an executable version is usually delivered on CD-ROM or DVD-ROM to the customer with an installation routine which installs the software onto the customer's computer. Explain what the installation routine does. [F452 Q2 Jan 2009 (6)]

Answers should include the following points

- The program is copied to a designated folder on the target computer
- Any necessary data files are copied
- Any necessary library files are copied and registered
- Shortcut / icon created to run the program easily
- User has the opportunity to configure program / run settings
- And configuration is saved in a file / registry
- Programs may need extracting from a compressed file

Index

%, 60

algorithm, 10
annotation, 79
argument, 25
array, 44
    declaring, 44
    defining, 45
    initialising, 46
    one dimension, 44
    serial searching, 46
    two dimensions, 44
ASCII, 64
assignment, 59

boolean, 43

char, 43
constant, 73

data
    borderline, 87
    invalid, 87
    normal, 87
date, 43
debugging
    breakpoints, 93
    compiler diagnostics, 93
    stepping, 93
    watches, 93
DIV, 60
dry run, 89

errors
    logic, 83
    run-time, 83
    syntax, 83
existence check, 70

files
    estimating size of, 53
    indexed sequential, 51
    random, 51
    retrieving, 52
    searching, 52
    sequential, 51
    serial, 51
    storing, 52
flowchart, 12
for-next, 31
format check, 70
function, 25

good interface design, 1
good program-writing techniques, 74, 77

identifier, 73
if-then, 28
if-then-else, 28
indentation, 80
indexed sequential files, 51
installation routine, 93
integer, 43
iteration, 25, 27
iterative development, 21

keyword, 73

length check, 70
logical operators
    AND, 61
    NOT, 61

Lightning Source UK Ltd.
Milton Keynes UK
UKOW03f2153120214

226376UK00007B/249/P